The Single-Parent Family in Children's Books:

An analysis and annotated bibliography, with an appendix on audiovisual material

by
Catherine Townsend Horner

The Scarecrow Press, Inc.
Metuchen, N.J. & London
1978

HQ
734
.H844

Library of Congress Cataloging in Publication Data

Horner, Catherine Townsend, 1937-
  The single-parent family in children's books.

  Includes indexes.
  1. Single-parent family. 2. Single-parent family--
Juvenile literature--Bibliography. I. Title.
HQ734.H844   016.30142'7   78-15403
ISBN 0-8108-1157-X

Copyright © 1978 by Catherine Townsend Horner

Manufactured in the United States of America

ACKNOWLEDGMENTS

for the complement of my two-parent family, Bert, Jane and Julia, for their assistance, encouragement, forbearance and fortitude, and for the other two Julies, Moore and Dalrymple, for their sine qua non support

TABLE OF CONTENTS

List of Tables	vii
Part I. INTRODUCTION	1
On Bibliotherapy	2
The Need for the Present Work	6
The Nature of the Research	8
References	12
Part II. THE ANALYSIS	15
General Aspects	15
Genre	17
Setting and Environment	20
Characterization	23
Style and Plot	28
Part III. CONCLUSIONS	32
The Summary	34
Part IV. EVALUATIVE CRITERIA with Coding Chart for All 215 Books	37
Part V. ANNOTATED BIBLIOGRAPHY (Classified by Cause of Single Parenthood)	
Widowhood	49
Divorce/Desertion/Separation	93
Orphan with Single Guardian	119
Protracted Absence of Parent(s)	133

Unwed/Indeterminable	143
Part VI. APPENDIX: AUDIOVISUAL MATERIAL	149
Distributors' Addresses	156
Index (to the Bibliography) by Predominant Parent	157
Author and Title Index (to the Bibliography)	165
Subject Index (to the Bibliography)	168

LIST OF TABLES
(All in Part II)

1	Audience	15
2	Preschool/primary analysis	16
3	Newbery analysis	16
4	Age distribution chart	17
5	Verisimilitude	18
6	Message	18
7	Period	19
8	Period analysis	20
9	Location	21
10	Milieu [class]	22
11	Ethnic minority	22
12	Reason [for single parenthood]	23
13	Widowhood analysis	24
14	Divorce/desertion/separation analysis	25
15	Parent/guardian	26
16	Parent analysis	27
17	Absent parent	28
18	Poverty analysis	28
19	Viewpoint analysis	29
20	Single parenthood as source of conflict	29
21	Change, adjustment	30

I

INTRODUCTION

Contrary to popular belief, the single-parent phenomenon was not a cataclysmic byproduct of the sexual revolution of the 1960's. Dr. Ernest R. Mowrer[1]* declared in 1927, for instance, that family disintegration (divorce, separation, and desertion) actually had its roots in the Reformation, which secularized marriage; in the Romantic movement, which ended parental domination of youth and patriarchal dominion over wives; and in the Industrial Revolution, which gave potential economic independence to women and created urban mobility and instability. He published statistics just as alarming then as those published today, indicating a 400 percent increase in the divorce rate between 1870 and 1924. By comparison, the divorce rate has merely tripled in the 49-year span between 1925 and 1974.[2]

On the other hand, beyond the shadow of a doubt, the single-parent family is a burgeoning microcosm of present Western society. While declining mortality rates have reduced the incidence of early widowhood, the rate of divorce and choice of alternative lifestyles have stepped in to overflow the breach. Indeed, divorce has become so commonplace in the United States that the United Methodist Church has recognized its reality and published a manual of divorce rites to release partners from their marriage vows, averring that "a divorce ritual is no more against marriage than a funeral is against life."[3]

American society forging into its third century is committed to human rights of every description, including women's, ethnic, sexual, and individual. Considering the rapid rise of the tide in this direction, society also recognizes the emotional need of all of its members, men, women, and children, to come to grips with these realities. The

---

*References will be found at the end of the chapter.

field of children's literature is keeping pace with these trends, as a heightened social and psychological concern for the child's welfare has developed among authors, as well as librarians, teachers, and psychologists.

On Bibliotherapy

What authors, critics, librarians and teachers do not agree upon is what constitutes realism? is it bibliotherapeutic? is bibliotherapy literature? and, in whose jurisdiction does bibliotherapy lie? Jane Langton[4] delineates three levels of verisimilitude in sanguinary detail: the superficial surface appearance; the layer of intense sensitivity below the quick; and the hardcore visceral level. She submits that a fiction writer chooses consciously or unconsciously to write at one or more of these levels; she prefers the middle ground. In cutting to the quick the author causes his readers to recognize their own feelings through a fictional character and also brings his story vividly to life, another meaning of the word quick.

Conversely, June Jordan[5] thinks that young people are the victims of reality both in books and in life. Sordidness is real, but it is only one aspect of reality, she asserts. When modern writers are admonished to be realistic, however, they are really being browbeaten to ignore the optimistic and accentuate the cynical or "to surrender to the unbearable." Reviewers applaud the pathological and pathogenic, coercing authors to invent tragedy instead of inventing solutions and uncovering genuine heroes and heroines, happiness and peace. She believes that 95 percent of what is written in the name of realism is "pointless, self-indulgent, status quo-protecting, and irresponsible garbage." Her prescription for the malaise is to support, invent, discover and develop good news about reality that will be self-perpetuating in the struggle for social change. If practicable and desirable alternatives to the present realism are not sought, humankind will wallow in self-fulfilling prophecy.

In concurrence, Eva Nelson,[6] a children's librarian, is distressed at the increasing use of unnecessary profanity in children's books since 1961. She states that the whole profession of juvenile librarianship is built on the premise that children's books do influence kids for good or evil, and that in the past the librarian's principle tenet was, "only the best is good enough for the young." Today when books appear

Introduction 3

with such vulgarities as "damn," "shit," and "my God" and no one lifts his pen in protest, the inference is that we should be "vastly relieved that another obsolete taboo" has been struck down. She queries, "Have all children's librarians concluded that it is our solemn duty to circulate profanity among children in order that none may grow up deprived?"

Norma Klein[7] rebuts by pleading guilty to expunging from her books four-letter words which she feels are important, because she knows that if she oversteps the bounds of some arbitrary standards of propriety she will lose readers. She also believes that to portray adult fallibility will not rob children of a sense of security. She appeals for books that will depict guiltless sex among young teens and picture books evincing the sexuality of children. Instead of striking down all values, she foresees the substitution of more intelligent, rational values for the traditional ones.

Death as the source of single parenthood parallels the course of human history, and Jane Abramson[8] writes that since Puritan times the treatment of the subject has evolved from an "obsessive preoccupation with death to an unhealthy avoidance of the inevitable." Today, however, just as birth and sex have become acceptable subjects for picture books and early readers, so juvenile literature is coming to grips with "the other fact of life--mortality." But, she cautions, fiction which is written deliberately to solve problems, whether of death or divorce, has the inherent pitfalls of contrived characterization and plot. Such anemic "problem books," she declares, can pass only for bibliotherapy, not literature.

Just as realism is argued vituperatively in literary circles, so bibliotherapy is open to many interpretations. Trends in bibliotherapy were assessed in 1962 by Ruth M. Tews,[9] and the composite definition at that time was very narrow and conservative:

> Bibliotherapy is a program of selected activity involving reading materials, planned, conducted, and controlled as treatment under the guidance of the physician for emotional and other problems. It must be administered by a skilled, professionally trained librarian within the prescribed purpose of goals. The important and dynamic factors are the relationships which are established, the patients' reactions and responses, and the reporting back

to the physician for interpretation, evaluation, and directions in follow-up.

The broadest of all interpretations of bibliotherapy holds that every didactic, value-enhancing component is bibliotherapeutic. In 1976 Mary Ellen Meegan[10] isolated a total of 39 such facets in second-grade literature. Among the most common are confidence, courage, frustration, ingenuity, patience and tolerance, looking beyond first impressions, cultural differences, adjusting and accepting, friendship, sharing, and certain aspects of family changes. She found that 92 percent of realistic fiction with bibliotherapeutic facets meet the criteria for good children's literature, and pack a moral punch in the bargain.

The American Library Association's handbook on bibliotherapy[11] favors a reasonably broad interpretation, noting the ancient origin of the practice. Aristotle believed that literature as well as other arts arouses emotions within individuals which have beneficial effects. Corinne W. Riggs[12] also invokes the Greeks who in classical times called the library the healing place of the soul. "For teachers and librarians bibliotherapy is simply the reading of books to aid in modifying the attitudes and behavior of boys and girls," she avows.

Carolyn T. Kingston[13] describes the school of thought that children should not be exposed to tragedy in books because adulthood with its serious problems lurks just around the corner, and the opposing philosophy that believes in early exposure and immunization to life's rawness with few holds barred, ignoring the risk of scarring. The conciliatory middle ground she proffers is a restatement of the ancient Greek insights: books for children that follow the design of classical tragedy with inherent aesthetic and emotional contributions, culminating in affirmation. Many books today masquerade as classical tragedy but lack the one necessary ingredient of catharsis, without which the story is a failure with a depressing aftertaste, a recital of adversity without design. Catharsis, as defined by the Greeks, is the spiritual cleansing that occurs through involvement in the suffering of another individual. Aristotle described literary tragedy as "an imitation of an action, both serious and having magnitude, complete in itself, presented in pleasurable language with incidents arousing pity and fear wherewith to accomplish a catharsis of these emotions." The emotional fears children face, the calamities in their lives, cannot be swept under the

Introduction

rug. Literary tragedy ameliorates them by showing children heroes who meet fears, loss, and death with inner strength and integrity. The fabric of literary tragedy is composed of conflict, climax, catharsis, elucidation, and finally, aesthetic statement. "Well-crafted tragedy pleases; it sings but does not hammer ... and children catch its melody."

But who is to administer bibliotherapy? Henry D. Olsen[14] says that bibliotherapy is "a process of dynamic interaction between literature and the reader's personality." It would follow that anyone with a knowledge of literature and an acquaintance with individual personalities or situations could apply it. The teacher, he concedes, will not approach bibliotherapy in the same manner as a bibliotherapist who deals with extreme cases, but he can certainly apply it as a preventive or therapeutic device upon minor social, emotional and psychological problems before they escalate.

This view does not dictate that the practitioner be a skilled therapist or zealous crusader, nor that the client be in need of drastic clinical treatment and control. It conveys the idea that teachers and librarians should be sensitized to the varying emotional and sociological needs of their clientele and be prepared and committed to help them identify, confront, and solve their problems through the recommendation of relevant reading material, dispensing a sort of preventive medicine in carefully measured doses of books to match their clients' symptoms.

Olsen expatiates on reading as superior to real-life situations, reasoning that "the reader can better accept unsavory appraisals of his weaknesses, since the mirror image does not threaten his ego directly."

Two non-fiction titles that are especially useful in helping intermediate age children to cope with the most common causes of single parenthood are Eda LeShan's <u>Learning to Say Good-by: When a Parent Dies</u>[15] which encourages the survivors to share their burden of grief, and Richard Gardner's older but still cogent <u>The Boys and Girls Book About Divorce</u>[16] which provides frank information and valid guidance for dealing with most conceivable divorce situations. Both books discuss remarriage. Another more recent title on divorce, Arlene Richards' <u>How to Get It Together When Your Parents Are Coming Apart</u>,[17] is addressed explicitly and forthrightly to adolescents from seventh grade up.

There will never be a resolution to the arguments raging around realism and bibliotherapy, but in the final analysis there is one incontrovertible admonition to which to adhere, aptly and bluntly stated by Alfred A. Arth and Judith D. Whittemore[18]:

> No teacher has the right to hand the child a book that tells of two parents taking a single child on a picnic in the country when in reality the student has only one parent at home and a picnic would be the last activity that family would choose for leisure time.

The Need for the Present Work

"If children do gain ideas and impressions about the world around them from the books they read ... it is surely important for adults to know what kind of world the books portray."[19] The foregoing is part of Tekla Bekkedal's closing statement from her 1973 study of 28 unpublished content analyses of the human relationships, values and cultural content, and racial and ethnic groups in children's literature. She disclosed one 1959 study of American family life as depicted in then-contemporary realistic children's fiction. A more recent content analysis of the image of the family on television programs and in young adult novels--in which the single-parent family was broached--was pursued at San Jose State University in 1975 by Mary E. Hustedt.[20] There have been several other recent research works at San Jose State including an annotated bibliography by Clara M. Latham,[21] which explores bibliotherapy for certain disturbed children and examines 65 titles involving adoption, divorce, stepparents, death of parent, and orphans; Beverly Loveland Nopola's[22] observations in depth of 30 selected titles on divorce in contemporary children's literature in 1975; and a study in 1970 by Regina Ball[23] of the relationship between school achievement and membership in a single-parent family. A spate of other published sources, some of them cited earlier in this paper, have truncated bibliographies of bibliotherapeutic books dealing with specific needs. None of them is comprehensive, exploratory, or exclusively single-parent oriented.

The Social Science Index, The Reader's Guide to Periodical Literature, and ERIC Resources in Education all have single-parent or one-parent families as descriptors, though only ERIC has listings pertaining to the children of such domiciles. In all other indexing and abstracting services the subject must be approached more generally and obliquely. Library Literature, for instance, classifies any pertinent publications under "Children's Reading--Psychological Aspects."

The Subject Guide to Books in Print names 16 adult titles on the single-parent family, ranging from a discursive technical treatise by a German psychologist and a survey descriptive analysis by British sociologists, to popular paperbacks and survival guides to parenting alone. The Subject Guide to Children's Books in Print has no such heading. The headings for death and orphans are not specific enough, and the heading for divorce in fiction enumerates only 11 titles.

And what of retrospective and out-of-print books? Bartlett C. Jones[24] in 1974 made rejoinder to feminists who castigate all existing children's literature for reinforcing stereotypical male/female roles by citing some old favorite heroines who are also assertive and aggressive, including Alice, Dorothy, Goldilocks, Madeline, the Little Red Hen, and Mike Mulligan's steam shovel Mary Ann! The single-parent family in children's fiction has been on the scene for generations, Heidi and The Five Little Peppers being two of the earliest, both published in 1880. Many others have gone out of print but have been retained on library shelves because of a still devoted following, and many have been resurrected in new editions as a new generation clamors for an old standby. Not all of the "oldies" are "goodies," but which are, and why, will be set forth.

The research that led to the writing of this book was founded on, and then substantiated, the feelings that, first, there has been a determined effort by the authors of children's fiction in the past decade (1966 to 1976) to write books for children depicting single-parent families realistically and forthrightly, and that, second, prior to 1966 the portrayal of fictional one-parent families was virtually non-existent for children under ten, and relevant titles for intermediate and junior high school children were moralistic period pieces or idealized adventure stories. One preconception was, however, shown to be wrong: pre-1966 titles for over-ten-year-olds relevant to the one-parent theme did <u>not</u> have a predominance of widowed mothers as that parent.

The Nature of the Research

Because this is an exploratory study in a field attracting considerable concerned attention today, breadth was considered of primary importance in achieving relevance and reliability. An attempt was made to identify as many as possible of the titles in children's fiction involving a single parent. Every volume of the Children's Catalog was scrutinized from recent supplements to the 1956 edition, probing each fiction and easy fiction annotation for clues suggesting single parenthood. The majority of these books of possible use were then located through the book catalog of the Santa Clara Valley Library System, California, one elementary and one junior high school library in San Jose's Alum Rock Union Elementary School District, as well as the library at San Jose State University.

Some books were eliminated from the list because they did not match the definition of single parenthood, broadly construed to be one adult acting in the capacity of parent or guardian to one or more children under 18 years of age for a protracted period of time. Other titles were stricken because they were simply unavailable for perusal during the research period, December 1976 through June 1977. Additional titles entailing single-parent situations obviously may have been overlooked because their annotations were too ambiguous to strike a responsive chord with the investigator, or they may never have appeared in the Children's Catalog. Some of these elusive ones were identified with the aid of obliging children's librarians, and some appeared serendipitously. The resulting sampling of 215 titles was sufficiently broad to be fully representative.

The content analysis method of investigation was chosen because of the exploratory nature of the study and the diversity of elements in the incidence of single parenthood in children's fiction. Bernard Berelson wrote in 1952 that "content analysis offers a sound approach to research on children's books because it is an objective, systematic, and quantitative method of describing content."[25] The investigation maintained as its goals all along the compilation under one cover of the pertinent attributes of this body of literature, and a discussion of the significance of the characters and the overall effectiveness of the titles, as well as a thoroughly annotated list of the books themselves. The present work provides a comprehensive view of the subject for adults (parents, psychologists, educators) who prepare and guide children through separation, bereavement, and traumatic upheavals in family structure, and for librarians who are interested in having a book collection that will support the efforts of these adults.

For pragmatic reasons, this study was limited to a single medium: fiction in book form. For a list of bibliotherapeutic resources in other media, see Part VI. Appendix.

Dates of publication were examined to differentiate works of the past decade from those of 1965 and earlier. The age of the intended readership was determined for each book, from preschool/primary to junior high, and the ages of the books' protagonists were posted when provided. No high school books were contemplated, and the term <u>young adult</u> was assiduously avoided as too ambiguous--encompassing, according to interpretation, anything "realistic" from prepubescence to full majority. Newbery and Caldecott medalists were denoted.

<u>Genre</u>

It is apparent that authors, critics, and librarians have widely divergent opinions of realism in children's fiction. Another authority, May Hill Arbuthnot,[26] defines realism simply as "a tale that is convincingly true to life; that is, the places, people, action, and motives seem both possible and plausible." For the purposes of this investigation it was necessary to make a further distinction between realism and idealism. A simple and objective if somewhat whimsical and unorthodox scheme was devised, the Alice-in-Wonderland principle. Alice, it will be recalled, experienced real difficulty and frustration in breaching the locked door she encountered in seeking entrance to the garden in Wonderland, being alternately too tall or too small. If the protagonist in the stories under consideration encountered closed doors at most critical junctures in the progression of the plot which fate, chance, or coincidence did not fling open for him in the nick of time, the plot was regarded as realistic. If, however, as he approached these obstacles, doors swung open for him providentially at the moment of truth, the book was deemed idealistic. Thus Sperry's <u>Call It Courage</u> with its beneficent albatross was judged idealistic, even though it abounds with immutable barriers. Books were also assigned to a third mutually exclusive category, that of fantasy, but few books proved to fall into this classification, because no folk or fairy tales or anthropomorphic animal stories were evaluated in the investigation.

    Period was also determined with distinctions made among historical fiction, period pieces, and contemporary literature. A contemporary setting was conceived to be one that transpired since 1960. Historical fiction had to be related to persons or events from recorded history, such as Corcoran's Axe-Time/Sword-Time which occurs at the outset of World War II. The category of period piece claimed the remainder.

    Two final elements of genre were identified, neither exclusive of the other. Moralism or didacticism, relatively simply to detect, needs no definition. Bibliotherapeutic value is a more elusive term, as earlier noted, but the definition utilized here has the merit of simplicity: any form of fiction has such a value if it has a capacity for constructive character formation or behavior modification. Evaline Ness' Sam, Bangs and Moonshine is both moralistic and bibliotherapeutic; Klein's Taking Sides is bibliotherapeutic alone; Spyri's Heidi is purely moralistic; while Flory's The Golden Venture is neither.

Setting and Environment

    For each book studied, the country in which the story transpires was designated, as was the general locality: urban, suburban/small town, or rural. A general assessment of social class was assigned. Upper class was interpreted to mean accustomed to affluence, as in Spykman's A Lemon and a Star. Middle class was expected to encompass the preponderance of the literature. Poverty in middle class (or even upper class) may be a temporary concern, but always there is the presence of a reasonable amount of education and cultural amenities. Estes' chronicles of the Moffat family are illustrative of this milieu. Lower class was characterized by poverty in combination with either a demonstrable lack of education and culture (not necessarily implying the absence of human dignity) as in Taylor's Teetoncey, or a slum or ghetto ambience as in Lexau's Me Day. Finally, ethnic minorities in the U.S. were identified with categories for black and Latin American, and a non-specific classification for other minorities that are designated by country of origin. Thus the Polish-American waif of Estes' The Hundred Dresses was recorded, as was Chinese-American Moon Shadow of Yep's memorable Dragonwings.

Introduction 11

Characterization

The reasons for single parenthood are sundry. As familiarity grew with the over two hundred works examined, causes were classified as widowhood, divorce/desertion/separation, orphaning (but with a single guardian), and the protracted absence of parent(s); an open-ended division was established for any others, such as the unwed mother of Klein's Mom, the Wolf Man and Me. The relationship of the single parent to the child was noted for each work, and when the absent parent appears in the story or is alluded to, the attitude displayed toward him or her was recorded. The element of poverty was again considered when a significant sacrifice in lifestyle was observed as in Sawyer's Year of Jubilo, in which the erstwhile upper-class family falls victim to straitened circumstances consistent with middle-class standards at the death of husband and father--circumstances with which they are singularly unsuited to cope, however. Thus poverty was judged as relative, not absolute, for the purpose of characterization.

Style and Plot

The viewpoint of each narrative was recorded to denote the first or third person idiom. Of particular concern to this investigation was the effect of the condition of single parenthood on the plot. Is the instance of single parenthood the source of primary conflict, as in Stolz' The Edge of Next Year, the source of secondary conflict, as in Bond's A String in the Harp, or is it incidental to the theme, as in Brink's Winter Cottage?

Also investigated, in fact one of the foremost issues of interest, was the reaction on the part of the children to the remarriage of their partnerless parent in applicable cases. Is the adjustment to the restructuring of the family unit relatively easy, as in Constant's Those Miller Girls, or relatively difficult, as in Cameron's A Room Made of Windows?

The evaluative criteria defined in the foregoing outline of the study are thus seen to lead from the general to the specific. The findings will be examined in the following analysis.

REFERENCES

[1] Mowrer, Ernest R. *Family Disorganization: An Introduction to a Sociological Analysis.* Chicago: University of Chicago Press, 1927; p. 4, 37.

[2] U.S. Bureau of the Census. *Statistical Abstract of the United States: 1975* (96th ed.). Washington, D.C., 1975; p. 51.

[3] *Ritual in a New Day: An Invitation.* Nashville, Tenn.: Abingdon Press, 1976.

[4] Langton, Jane. "Down to the Quick: The Use of Daily Reality in Writing Fiction," *Horn Book* 49:24-30, February 1973.

[5] Jordan, June. "Young People: Victims of Realism in Books and in Life," *Wilson Library Bulletin* 48:140-5, October 1973.

[6] Nelson, Eva. "Take Cuss Words out of Kids' Books," *Wilson Library Bulletin* 49:32-3, October 1974.

[7] Klein, Norma. "More Realism for Children," *Top of the News* 31:307-12, April 1975.

[8] Abramson, Jane. "Facing the Other Fact of Life: Death in Recent Children's Fiction," *School Library Journal* 99:3257-9, December 15, 1974.

[9] Tews, Ruth M. "Trends in Bibliotherapy," *Library Trends* 11:97-105, October 1962.

[10] Meegan, Mary Ellen. "Bibliotherapeutic Facets in Literature for Children." Doctoral dissertation, Boston College, 1976.

[11] Association of Hospital and Institutional Libraries. *Bibliotherapy: Methods and Materials.* Chicago: American Library Association, 1971; p. 3.

[12] Riggs, Corinne W. *Bibliotherapy: An Annotated Bibliography.* Newark, Del.: International Reading Association, 1971; p. 1.

[13] Kingston, Carolyn T. *The Tragic Mode in Children's*

Literature. New York: Teachers College Press, 1974; p. 1-4.

[14] Olsen, Henry D. "Bibliotherapy to Help Children Solve Problems," Elementary School Journal 75:422-9, April 1975.

[15] LeShan, Eda. Learning to Say Good-by: When a Parent Dies. New York: Macmillan, 1976.

[16] Gardner, Richard A. The Boys and Girls Book about Divorce. New York: Jason Aronson, 1970.

[17] Richards, Arlene, and Irene Willis. How to Get It Together When Your Parents Are Coming Apart. New York: David McKay, 1976.

[18] Arth, Alfred A., and Judith D. Whittemore. "Selecting Literature for Children That Relates to Life, the Way It Is," Elementary English 50:726-8+, May 1973.

[19] Bekkedal, Tekla. "Content Analysis of Children's Books," Library Trends 22:109-26, October 1973.

[20] Hustedt, Mary E. "The Family: A Content Analysis," San Jose State University, Department of Librarianship, research paper no. 628, 1975.

[21] Latham, Clara Mildred. "Bibliotherapy for Certain Disturbed Children," San Jose State University, Department of Librarianship, research paper no. 713, 1975.

[22] Nopola, Beverly Loveland. "The Representation of Divorce in Contemporary Children's Literature: A Content Analysis," San Jose State University, Department of Librarianship, research paper no. 703, 1975.

[23] Ball, Regina. "A Study of the Relationship between School Achievement and Membership in a One-Parent Family." Thesis, San Jose State University, 1970.

[24] Jones, Bartlett C. "A New Cache of Liberated Children's Literature--In Some Old Standbys!" Wilson Library Bulletin 49:52-6, September 1974.

[25] Quoted in Bekkedal [reference 19].

[26] Arbuthnot, May Hill. *Children and Books.* Chicago: Scott, Foresman, 1957; p. 392.

II

THE ANALYSIS

The single-parent family is alive and proliferating in children's fiction, from the "Three M Company" of Malones, Melendys and Moffats who so humorously and adroitly slew the dragons of the 1940's, to troubled Chloris of the 1970's who creates conflicts instead of resolving them. A total of 215 titles were perused, analyzed and annotated for inclusion in these pages, by no means a complete compilation. Numbers appearing in brackets refer the reader to entries in the Annotated Bibliography (as well as entries in the Evaluative Criteria chart, Part IV).

General Aspects

Of the 215 books, 41 percent were originally published in or before 1965; the remainder, 59 percent, were copyrighted from 1966 to 1976. The preponderance, 58 percent, are of course geared to the intermediate level; only 18, or 8 percent, were identified as preschool/primary, a paltry three predating 1966, but a salubrious 73 were found on the junior high level, 68 percent of which were written in 1966 and after (Table 1). Grade levels are not to be considered absolute, but assignment of general reading level, however subjectively done, was thought to be necessary. Consult the

Table 1. Audience	Pre-1966†	Post-1966†	Total
Preschool/primary	3	15	18
Intermediate	62	62	124
Junior high	23	50	73
Total	88	127	215

†For the purposes of the tables in this analysis chapter, "pre-1966" is to be understood as through 1965; "post-1966," then, begins with the year 1966.

Annotated Bibliography for recommended grade level as well as ages of protagonists.

A closer examination of preschool/primary titles disclosed that in both pre-1966 households headed by females, Martin and Abraham Lincoln [191] and Benjie [168], poverty was indicated; the latter title represented a black household (see Table 2). Neither widowhood nor divorce was specified as the cause of single parenthood in any of the three pre-1966 books, while divorce accounted for eight and widowhood only three of the 15 titles in 1966 and after. Minority representation since 1966 in picture books scored one third of the total. Likewise, Joan M. Lexau and Charlotte Zolotow were responsible for producing one third of the easy books.

Table 2.

Preschool/primary analysis	Pre-1966	Post-1966	Total
Total	3	15	18
Widowhood	0	3	3
Divorce	0	8	8
Female head	2	12	14
Minority	1	6	7
Poverty	2	4	6

Newbery Medalists accounted for 11 of the titles, an astonishing seven of which belong to the earlier period. Another indication that Newbery Medalists have been precursors of social trends is the fact that of the 11, eight were of a pluralistic nature with such diverse demographic heroes as Bulgarian peasant Dobry [72], Young Fu of Chungking [61], Spanish Manolo [95], British troubador Adam [206], Incan Cusi [159], and Polynesian Mafatu [75]. Bibliotherapy and the manifestation of poverty among the 11 was equally divided between the two periods, but realism was observed more frequently since 1966 (see Table 3). Caldecott Medalists held no distinctions in the single-parent genus as only two books were found, the fantasy Many Moons [210] and the realistic Sam, Bangs and Moonshine [67].

Table 3. Newbery analysis	Pre-1966	Post-1966	Total
Total	7	4	11
Pluralism	6	2	8
Realism	2	4	6
Bibliotherapy	3	3	6
Poverty	2	2	4

Table 4. Age distribution chart

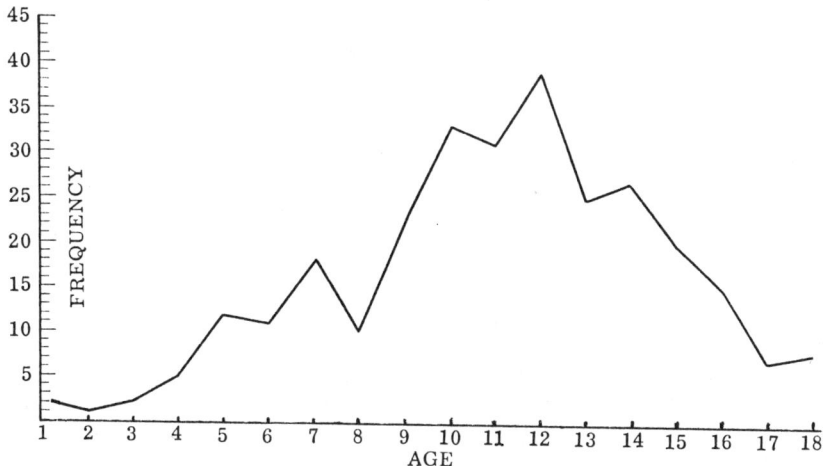

The age of protagonists of preschool/primary stories was usually indeterminable, so the ages in the age distribution chart (Table 4) may be slightly weighted in favor of older children, but there are sufficient indeterminable ages in the older ranks to offset the small number of picture books. An effort was made to determine the ages of all the children in the family even though one child may have dominated the story. If the book encompassed more than one year of the child's life, his age at the outset was considered official with the exceptions of Nino [184] and The Children on the Top Floor [176], those unwanted babes so generously bequeathed to egocentric television personality Malcolm Master on Christmas Eve, in which the terminal age was used.

Genre

The occurrence of realism was roughly the same as that of idealism, by **47** vs. **45** percent, but the distribution by publication date was widely dichotomous, with **76** percent of the **1966** and after titles identified as realistic, as opposed to **24** percent of the earlier books, Vera and Bill Cleaver marching in the vanguard (see Table 5). Fantasy was represented by 18 titles, including some provocative science fiction such as A Wrinkle in Time [196], A String in the Harp [5], and The Prince in Waiting [16] in which Luke witnesses the foul murder of first one and then the other parent in a future feudalistic state.

Table 5. Verisimilitude	Pre-1966	Post-1966	Total
Realism	24	76	100
Idealism	56	41	97
Fantasy	8	10	18
Total	88	127	215

Only 15 percent of post-1966 fiction was classified as moralistic, while 80 percent was adjudged to be bibliotherapeutic, confirming pre-investigation expectations (see Table 6). Of the total 27 moralistic tales, eight were also found to be bibliotherapeutic, almost all predating 1966, including The World of Ellen March [112]. Even the lachrymal sexagenarian, The Secret Garden [157], has its bibliotherapeutic element. Many bibliotherapeutic titles contained therapeutic facets quite unrelated to single parenthood. Trouble on Treat Street [151], which deals with race relationships, and I Would Rather Be a Turnip [19], which treats of illegitimacy, are illustrative. A complement of 116 bibliotherapeutic books was recorded, some in the tragic Greek mode--e.g., The Bears' House [141] in which the mother becomes psychotic following her husband's desertion and the family ultimately dissolves-- and others as heartwarming as A Book for Jodan [132] wherein the protagonist's sensitive divorced dad creates a highly personal scrapbook for her of shared experiences and emotions that diminishes the distance between them.

Table 6. Message*	Pre-1966	Post-1966	Total
Moralism	23	4	27
Bibliotherapy	23	93	116
Neither	48	32	80
Total	94	129	223

*May be more than one.

Of the 80 books assessed as neither moralistic nor bibliotherapeutic, 60 percent existed from the earlier period. They were chiefly humor or adventure stories in which single parenthood was incidental to the plot. Danny the Champion of the World [25] is an audacious example as he displays his prowess at poaching pheasants from apoplectic Squire Hazel; others are Gabriel [30], a dog story, or Star Bright [50], a horse story. Most are retrospective as in Swallows and Amazons [197], an idyllic, nautical summer vacation adventure, or A Touch of Magic [15], a tale of the American Revolution based on the lives of the legendary Shippen girls of Philadelphia.

The Analysis 19

Realism and bibliotherapy will be treated at greater length in succeeding paragraphs.

More than half of all the books, 55 percent, were contemporary, while 17 percent were clearly identified as historical fiction, and the remaining 27 percent were designated period pieces (see Table 7). Because all titles written prior to 1960, not otherwise labeled as historical, were considered period pieces even though they were intended to be contemporary at their time of publication, an inflated 76 percent of the 59 period pieces is thus attributable to the pre-1966 period. These embraced some of the best traditional single-parent fare for children, including two of the droll Moffat series [37 etc.] and two of the Melendy family saga [33 etc.].

Table 7. Period	Pre-1966	Post-1966	Total
Contemporary	21	98	119
Historical fiction	22	14	36
Period piece	45	14	59
Total	88	126*	214*

*One not applicable.

Predictably, 82 percent of the 119 contemporary stories belonged to the later period (see Table 8), but the 28 combined retrospective titles (historical and period) produced since 1966 comprised some excellent fiction that was both realistic and bibliotherapeutic, among them The Garden Is Doing Fine [41], a poignant narrative of terminal illness, and Give Dad My Best [192], an equally stirring chronicle of family dissolution. The pre-1966 period was not moribund, however, maintaining a full half of the 52 realistic and bibliotherapeutic titles with such memorable books as the World War II aftermath story, The Ark [187], and Shadow of a Bull [95], as well as those of more dubious distinction such as the saintly Stepsister Sally [28] or The Grizzly [121] which, while ascribed as realistic, was not considered bibliotherapeutic because of David's unrealistic expectation that his parents will be reconciled. Not to be overlooked were yarns of the post-1966 period written retrospectively in a lighter vein, among them the vibrant and puckish Chancy and the Grand Rascal [162] and Me, California Perkins [99], a story of desert silver mining days.

Table 8. Period analysis	Pre-1966	Post-1966	Total
Total contemporary	21	98	119
Contemporary realism	10	64	74
Contemporary bibliotherapy	10	80	90
Total retrospective	67	28	95
Retrospective realism	14	12	26
Retrospective bibliotherapy	13	13	26
Retrospective poverty	23	15	38

The representation of poverty in all historical and period (retrospective) titles was measured in the vague expectation of seeing a greater incidence of the depiction of poverty in books published in and after 1966, but the correlation was negative because of the overwhelming numbers of pre-1966 retrospective titles, 71 percent of the total (Table 8). Proportionally, however, the post-1966 era made a stronger showing of "telling it like it is" (or in this case "was") by demonstrating poverty in 54 percent of its retrospective titles, compared to 34 percent of its pre-1966 counterparts. Poverty will be studied in greater depth presently.

Setting and Environment

It came as no surprise to find that 74 percent of all stories were set in the United States, with 64 percent of the total, both contemporary and retrospective, belonging to the post-1966 period. Miscellaneous other countries were represented, 62 percent of them by pre-1966 authors, reflecting the earlier Newbery statistics and indicative of John Rowe Townsend's statement in the June 1977 Horn Book that he hears from librarians in both England and America that children are resistant to foreign books and that more and more British books, even, will fail to cross the Atlantic. ["Peering into the Fog: The Future of Children's Books," 53:346-55]. England, quite naturally, contributed the most, with 15 titles from the antediluvian melodrama, A Little Princess [10], 1892, to the latest humorous adventure, Danny the Champion of the World [25], 1975. Sweden followed with five rather progressive titles, including The Night Daddy [207] and Lillan [133]. That number would have swelled but for the inadvertent omission of the marginally single-parent Pippi Longstocking books by Astrid Lindgren. Scotland, France, Germany, Denmark, Switzerland, and Spain registered two apiece. Thirteen other countries as disparate as Greenland,

Angola, and Australia accounted for the remainder of the total of 45. Only 11 books failed to identify nationality, seven of them preschool/primary.

A dramatic 80 percent of all stories with urban settings occurred in the post-1966 period, but urban settings accounted for only 26 percent of titles overall. As anticipated, 40 percent of all books evinced a suburban/small town locality, 41 percent of this number dealing with the pre-1966 era (see Table 9). The pre-1966 era, however, did have a disproportionate number of rural locales with 56 percent of the total 71. Four, two from each period, were indeterminable or not applicable, such as Peter Treegate's War [212], a story of the American Revolution, while two, Three on the Run [2], a British adventure, and Taking Sides [124], a modern divorce theme, were so evenly divided in locale that they were coded twice.

Table 9. Location*	Pre-1966	Post-1966	Total
Urban	11	44	55
Suburban/small town	36	51	87
Rural	40	31	71
Indeterminable/inapplicable	2	2	4
Total	89	128	217

*May be more than one.

Middle class registered an overwhelming plurality in milieu with 62 percent of all titles, as predicted; 43 percent are ascribed to the pre-1966 period (see Table 10). Lower class followed with 24 percent of the total, but its trend mirrored that of urbanization with 73 percent of this number appearing since 1966. Upper-class ambience was evenly divided; 15 titles appeared in each period. Five books were listed twice because they involved two different families of digressive situation, including The Witches of Barguzin [87], a grisly but poignant Russian love story, Lady Ellen Grae [104], who is sent to live with her wealthy aunt to learn social graces, Devil in the Fog [47], a tale of eighteenth-century British intrigue, and Time at the Top [68] and its sequel All in Good Time [69], delicious science fiction confections. In both African titles, Meeting with a Stranger [188] and The Wilderness Has Ears [91], and the Greenland saga, Eskimo Boy [46], class was deemed not applicable.

22   The Single-Parent Family

Table 10. Milieu*	Pre-1966	Post-1966	Total
Upper class	15	16	31
Middle class	57	77	134
Lower class	14	37	51
Not applicable	2	1	3
Total	88	131	219

*May be more than one.

Ethnicity was measured in the U.S. only and was extended to include not only the protagonist and his blood family but best friends, close associates and stepfamily (see Table 11). Thus disturbed Chloris [139, 140], whose mother marries a Chicano, was considered ethnic minority, as was The Egypt Game [74] in which April's best friends are a black and an Oriental; This Is a Recording [107] and The Slave Dancer [45] in which the protagonists have initially unpleasant but unavoidably close encounters with, respectively, American Indians and African slaves; and What It's All About [125] wherein the family adopts a Vietnamese orphan.

Blacks led the list with 19 citations, all but two of them, Benjie [168] and Shuttered Windows [171], written since 1966. All eight titles entailing Latin Americans appeared since 1966. Five preschool/primary books depicted blacks and one portrayed Latin Americans, Friday Night Is Papa Night [199], in which young Pedro is the only one awake to welcome Papa on his return from a weary week of moonlighting. Another 14 represented assorted minorities, five of them in existence in 1965. The most frequent unspecified minority was the American Indian with five citations, three of them predating 1966 which were somewhat mawkish, especially Chi-Wee [65]. Italian and Chinese Americans claimed two each with a single representation for Polish, Vietnamese, Irish, and Jewish Americans. The latter, Thank You, Jackie Robinson [21], was, like The Egypt Game, posted twice because of Sam's relationship with an elderly black. Trouble on Treat Street [151] was also double coded for the friendship that develops between a black and a Chicano boy.

Table 11. Ethnic minority*	Pre-1966	Post-1966	Total
Black	2	17	19
Latin American	0	8	8
Other minorities	5	8	13
Total	7	33	40

*May be more than one.

Of the total of 40 minority citations, 25 were deemed to be realistic, including a scant four from the early period (Table 15). Another 27 were designated bibliotherapeutic of which just three existed prior to 1965, The Hundred Dresses [205], Shuttered Windows [171], and Benjie [168].

Characterization

The causes of single parenthood ranged from the bizarre Moses-in-the-bulrushes advent of baby John Thomas to misanthropic Luke Vail in White Bird [155] to the immutable incidence of the unwed mother as in Ludell [213] and others, but early widowhood remained the strongest faction in children's fiction, if not in reality, with 46 percent of the total, of which a majority, 55 percent, pertained to the pre-1966 era (see Table 12). The figures reveal, however, that only nine of the 54 earlier titles contained the quality of realism, a dismal 17 percent, while 11 more had bibliotherapeutic facets (see Table 13). The Moffats and Melendys may be entertaining, but they are not particularly useful for problem solving, if that is the desired goal.

Table 12. Reason*	Pre-1966	Post-1966	Total
Widowhood	54	45	99
Divorce/desertion/separation	3	56	59
Orphan	17	14	31
Protracted absence	14	18	32
Other/indeterminable	5	8	13
Total	93	141	234

*For single parenthood; may be more than one.

One revelatory and unexpected set of statistics brought the startling realization that widowers outnumbered widows in both periods by a nearly identical 54 percent for early fiction and 53 percent for recent fiction! One might speculate that the phenomenon of motherlessness prior to 1966 reflects the authors' respect for the ravages of childbirth and disease before the advancement of medical science and the rigors of farm and homelife before widespread automation. For the later period it is easy to speculate that contemporary authors did not feel the constraint of convention in choosing the less orthodox of the two parents, i.e., the father, to rear the children, as in Portrait of Ivan [44], Sasha My Friend [24], or Grover [18], another case of terminal illness combined with suicide. Of course, the proliferation of retrospective

titles occurring in the post-1966 period would also tend to
swell the ranks of widowers if the earlier premise is true
that life took a greater toll of young mothers than fathers
fictionally as well as historically.

Table 13. Widowhood analysis	Pre-1966	Post-1966	Total
Total Widowhood	54	45	99
Realism	9	24	33
Bibliotherapy	11	27	38
Mother parent	25	21	46
Father parent	29	24	53

Only two preschool/primary books specified widowhood
as cause of single parenthood, both motherless, Sam, Bangs
and Moonshine [67] and "Hey, What's Wrong with This One?"
[94]. Of the two, only the former portrayed a serious, distressful situation. The latter, however, tempers with levity
a frequently somber subject.

The divorced/deserted/separated composed the second
greatest phalanx of single parents, claiming 27 percent, with
an astonishing escalation in new titles over the past decade
from three to 56. A healthy 75 percent of the post-1966 books
displayed realism, while a full 91 percent contained bibliotherapeutic elements (see Table 4). One title was entirely
too realistic to be therapeutic except in a controlled, structured session, When the Sad One Comes to Stay [119], in
which Sara accepts the spurious expediency and loses her own
identity. Representing the full panoply of situations, the books
in this category ranged from the amicable, civilized type of
parental relationships of The Telltale Summer of Tina C.
[135] and Ellen Grae [103] to the caustic, depredatory relationships of Heads You Win; Tails I Lose [120] or The Boy
Who Could Make Himself Disappear [138]; from the abject
squalor of The Bears' House [141] and Don't Look and It
Won't Hurt [134] to the luxury and affluence of Boy on the
Run [102] and Axe-Time/Sword-Time [105]; and from the arcane art of French cookery in It's Not What You Expect [123]
to the less sublime refinements of Little League baseball in
Matt Gargan's Boy [142].

The Analysis

Table 14. D/D/S analysis*	Pre-1966	Post-1966	Total
Total	3	56	59
Realism	2	42	44
Bibliotherapy	1	51	52
Mother parent	3	45	48
Father parent	0	12	12

*Divorce/desertion/separation.

It is unremarkable that all three applicable titles before 1965 gave mothers custody, nor that 80 percent of the later titles followed suit. As Jeff's dad in A Month of Sundays [100] succinctly expresses it, "... most children live with their mothers if their parents aren't together."

There was a total of eight preschool/primary books dealing with divorce or desertion of which three were of blacks and two depicted ghetto conditions with the father absent, J. T. [148] and Me Day [127].

Protracted absence accounted for 15 percent of all titles and represented a plethora of common and uncommon experiences, including wartime separation: Martin and Abraham Lincoln [191], Dark Dreams [198], The Ark [187], The Bells of Bleecker Street [183], and The Mitchells [201]; incarceration: Queenie Peavy [189] and Sounder [185]; emigration: Nino [184] and A Papa Like Everyone Else [200]; and immigration: Dragonwings [202]. Forty-four percent existed before 1966; since then there have been 18 more titles.

Orphan stories appeared to be on the decline, however, at least those of a single-parent nature. Of the total of 31, only 14 were published in the last decade. Boys continued to outnumber girls as protagonists, while uncles slightly outweighed grandmothers and unrelated males as preferred guardians, as in Big Blue Island [164] and Peachtree Island [167], uncles with a male and female ward, respectively.

An open-ended category recorded the condition of unwed mother and single parenthood of indeterminable origin, a total of 13 (unwed mothers accounting for three of these). Four of the indeterminable nine were in preschool/primary books.

Many single-parent titles defied categorization under one predominant parent and had to be double coded, typified by Up a Road Slowly [56] and The Summer of the Swans [11] in which the widowed fathers entrust the children to their aunts' guardianship, or Ann Aurelia and Dorothy [190] wherein A. A.'s mother places her in a foster home so she can remarry. This double coding is likely to cause some distortion among the following and foregoing figures and may be construed as equivocation, but who is to choose between the natural parent and the surrogate. It requires a more discriminating arbiter than this investigator.

One versatile title is a requisite for the institution with a truncated budget. Marinka, Katinka and Me (Susie) [62] are fourth-grade friends living with their natural mothers; Marinka's parents are divorced, Katinka's father is in prison, while Susie's dad is dead. For good measure, the bibliotherapeutic theme of a friendship triangle was provided.

In correlation with previous tallies, the total number of mother-oriented households exceeded that of father-oriented ones by 53 to 33 percent, but there was a dramatic gain by mothers as realism became entrenched after 1966, registering 68 percent of the 115 titles in the later period (see Table 15). Fathers, contrariwise, headed 47 percent of 72 homes in the books of 1965 and before but made a small gain of only four titles in the subsequent decade. Related and unrelated females also jumped boldly in the post-1966 period, while both related and unrelated males slumped abysmally. This is probably a reflection of the American social welfare system which has tended to award the child to the purportedly more wholesome and stable environment provided by a woman, but there were at least three books in the post-1966 period that go against this belief--First Step [144], Garden of Broken Glass [131], and Listen for the Fig Tree [63]--in all of which maternal alcoholism and deplorable poverty are handmaidens.

Table 15.

Parent/guardian*	Pre-1966	Post-1966	Total
Mother	37	78	115
Father	34	38	72
Related female	8	18	26
Related male	8	3	11
Unrelated female	3	6	9
Unrelated male	6	1	7
Total	96	144	240

*May be more than one.

The comparison of realism and bibliotherapeutic value between all female heads of household and their male counterparts (Table 16) reveals that while both groups made colossal proportionate gains in both realism and bibliotherapeutic value after 1966, there is a negative correlation between the two groups before 1965. Male heads of household posted more realistic titles but fewer bibliotherapeutic ones, while females registered lower realism but higher bibliotherapy, much of which also paraded as moralism, tending to affirm an initial expectation for finding a predominance of uncomplicated adventure stories for boys and benign period pieces for girls.

Table 16. Parent analysis	Pre-1966	Post-1966	Total
Total realism*	27	88	115
Male parent realism	14	28	42
Female parent realism	13	60	73
Total bibliotherapy*	26	108	134
Male parent bibliotherapy	11	28	39
Female parent bibliotherapy	15	80	95

*Figures adjusted to reflect multiple coding and do not tally with Tables 6 and 7.

The absent parent was portrayed or alluded to sympathetically in 48 percent of all the books, a commensurate number of times in each period (see Table 17), but while only two pre-1966 titles treated the missing parent unfavorably--The Long Secret [113], with its flamboyant, sybaritic, contemporary mother, and Two Logs Crossing [32], with its slothful, improvident, retrospective father--18 more burst into publication in the succeeding decade, a burgeoning exposure to reality.

A neutral classification was established expressly for parents who displayed both odious and redeeming qualities and for orphans and others whose missing parents balanced one another, as in The Barrel [179] in which Chance's boastful, egotistic father indirectly caused his gentle wife's death. Neutrality claimed 23 titles in the later period, as opposed to five in the earlier period.

In a full 30 percent of all titles, however, the absent parent was simply not alluded to at all or was mentioned so briefly or ambiguously that it was not possible to make a judgment. Calculably, the preponderance of these, 59 percent, occurred before 1966 when fictional life inclined to continue blithely without the missing "loved one." Preschool/primary books accounted for eight indeterminables, only one, however, coming from the earlier period, Many Moons [210].

Table 17. Absent parent	Pre-1966	Post-1966	Total
Sympathetic	43	60	103
Unsympathetic	2	18	20
Neutral	5	23	28
Not mentioned/indeterminable	38	26	64
Total	88	127	215

Demonstrable poverty was present in 29 percent of the books, roughly proportionately divided between pre-1966 (44 percent) and post-1966 (56 percent); deeper analysis disclosed that of the 28 pre-1966 titles, only nine combined poverty and realism, and an even more minuscule seven displayed bibliotherapeutic aspects.

The "poor widow" image of pre-1966 was observed in 19 titles in which a female was head of household (see Table 18). Male heads of household where poverty prevailed were limited to ten before 1966 and dropped to eight in the past decade, while impoverished female heads of household hurtled to 29, or 46 percent, of the total poverty stories. The incidence of minority male parent poverty increased from a lone title in 1965, the Polish-American father of The Hundred Dresses [205], to a mere two since 1966, notably the Chinese-American Dragonwings [202]. Minority female poverty rose from five titles in the early period to 14 new ones, paralleling the social order.

Table 18. Poverty analysis	Pre-1966	Post-1966	Total
Total	28	35	63
Realism	9	23	32
Bibliotherapy	7	25	32
Female parent	19	29	48
Male parent	10	8	18
Minority female parent	5	14	19
Minority male parent	1	2	3

Style and Plot

Use of the first person singular or diary style was an embryonic idiom in children's fiction prior to 1966; it was observed only five times in that period but 41 times in the succeeding decade. The viewpoint was measured in this investigation in anticipation that the use of a first-person style in a book would accompany a higher degree of realism and bibliotherapy than the 215 books as a whole would show. Tabulations confirmed that 72 percent of the first-person viewpoint in single parenthood was realistic, but that only 59 percent of it was bibliotherapeutic (see Table 18). The general population indicated an incidence of 47 percent realism and 54 percent bibliotherapy. While use of the first person seems successful in creating realism, it was not quite so laudatory for the purpose of writing books useful in bibliotherapy. Four fantasies, Eyes in the Fishbowl [145], The Prince in Waiting [16], The Sherwood Ring [173], and A Father Like That [150], were written in first person, only the latter bibliotherapeutic.

Table 19. Viewpoint analysis	Pre-1966	Post-1966	Total
Total first person	5	41	46
First person realism	2	31	33
Total realism	24	76	100
First person bibliotherapy	1	26	27
Total bibliotherapy	23	93	116

A major goal of this study was to identify those books in which the condition of single parenthood was the primary or secondary conflict in hopes of elucidating those which spoke specifically to that phenomenon. A significant 36 percent-- 77 titles, 61 from the later period--evinced primary conflict, while another 45, more equably divided between periods, demonstrated secondary conflict (see Table 20). In It's Not the End of the World [101], Karen's parents' divorce is patently the primary conflict, while in Heads You Win; Tails I Lose [120], Melissa, tormented and stultified by her parents' vitriolic verbal duels, actually importunes them to get divorced, a secondary conflict to her drug dependence. In 43 percent of the books, of which 57 percent existed in 1965, single parenthood caused insignificant emotional conflict.

Table 20. Single parenthood As source of conflict	Pre-1966	Post-1966	Total
Primary conflict	16	61	77
Secondary conflict	19	26	45
Insignificant conflict	53	40	93
Total	88	127	215

Closely allied was the measurement of remarriage and
reconciliation (in Table 21). This category claimed a number
that registered insignificant conflict to the condition of single
parenthood, but when that parent or even the absent parent
upset the status quo by remarrying, it often had a deleterious
effect on the children, as in Guy Lenny [130] who even contemplates suicide. Of the 42 episodes of remarriage/reconciliation, 74 percent of them from the past decade, the adjustment
to the change of status was assessed to determine if it was
relatively easy or difficult. In three instances the children
actively connive to get their widowed fathers espoused again,
one from the early period, Those Miller Girls! [22], and
two from the later period, All in Good Time [69] and "Hey,
What's Wrong with This One?" [94]. Reconciliations are effected in three others, all post-1966, It's Not What You Expect [123], Me, California Perkins [99], and Shadow on the
Water [97]. Of the 14 easy adjustments, nine occurred in
books published in 1966 and after, but of the 27 more difficult
adjustments, 21 or 78 percent occurred post-1966.

Table 21. Change, adjustment	Pre-1966	Post-1966	Total
Total change	88	127	215
Remarriage/reconciliation	11	31	42
Not applicable	77	96	173
Total adjustment	11	30	41
Relatively easy	5	9	14
Relatively difficult	6	21	27
Adjustment realism	4	18	22
Adjustment bibliotherapy	6	23	29

A closer evaluation of adjustment revealed that a feeble
10 percent of remarriage situations prior to 1966 were also
realistic, while 15 percent were bibliotherapeutic. The post-
1966 period posted an improved 44 percent rate of realism
and a 56 percent rate of bibliotherapy. Remarriage was
evinced in only two preschool/primary books, "Hey, What's
Wrong with This One?" [94], neither realistic nor bibliotherapeutic, and Eliza's Daddy [147], idealistic but bibliotherapeutic,
depicting a middle-class black girl whose divorced father has
remarried and inherited a stepdaughter about her age. Diffident Eliza dreams that her stepsister is a "Wonderful Angel
Daughter" who will supersede her in Daddy's affections, but
her fears are allayed and they both share good times with
Daddy.

And thus it is with the single-parent family in children's literature. <u>Heidi</u> [175] and <u>The Five Little Peppers</u> [73] retain their niche in children's affections, as do the Moffats and Melendys, the adventure, the humor, and the retrospection. They have not all been deposed in disgrace by books of uncompromising social concern, although these, epitomized by <u>Eliza's Daddy</u> [147], have displayed a vigorous upsurgence since 1966. There is a need and a place for both in harmonious juxtaposition to provide good times with reading.

III

CONCLUSIONS

The single-parent family in children's literature has been remarkable for both its diversity and specificity, from A Home with Aunt Florry [177] in her eccentric warehouse-cum-pigeon cote to Jane Hope [49], that encomium to the sedate antebellum South; from the humorous fantasy of The Mummy Market [204] to the agonizing pathos of The Garden Is Doing Fine [41]; from the adrenalin-charged historical adventure The Year of the Bloody Sevens [78] to the introspective ruminations of A Girl Called Al [117], which tackles contemporary divorce problems with drollery.

Many books evoked comparison because of the similar propensities they displayed. In Wind in the Chimney [64] and Apple Tree Cottage [85], the respectively fatherless and motherless families move into deserted Pennsylvania farmhouses where they are suffered to remain by virtue of their own industry and the magnanimity of their landlords. Nino [184], Dobry [72], and A Papa Like Everyone Else [200] are paeans to peasant village life in bucolic European locales. The boy of City in the Winter [209] spends a snowy day with his grandmother and working mother in their apartment, while the boy of The Sky Dog [211] spends a whimsical summer vacation with his mother at the beach; both are picture books.

Two grieving professional fathers, a doctor in Witch of the Cumberlands [79] and a professor in A String in the Harp [5], take their families to remote, foreboding locations following the mothers' deaths where the children incite adventure entailing local history and supernatural manifestations. The ESP theme was also shared by My Brother Angel [3], the eerie and sinister Down a Dark Hall [31], A Gift of Magic [109], and The Witch's Daughter [152]. Ghosts stalk the pages of The Figure in the Shadows [153], Eyes in the Fishbowl [145], The Sherwood Ring [173], and The Ghosts [1].

Conclusions 33

Manolo of Shadow of a Bull [95] seems destined to follow his father as a torero, a fate he abhors and which his mother is resignedly powerless to avert, while Rudi of Banner in the Sky [84] yearns to surpass his father's mountaineering feats which his mother has abjured him from doing. Both fathers lost their lives to their vocations. Rudi wins the right to pursue his destiny with his mother's blessing, while Manolo earns the right to repudiate it without disgracing his mother.

Several protagonists find their callings in the Arts: Maria Lupin [194] in music, Kirby of A Gift of Magic [109] in dance, Kit of The Beauty Queen [136] in drama, Dobry [72] in art, and Julia of A Room Made of Windows [12] and Bridie of A Sound of Chariots [57] in letters. The fathers of White Twilight [70] and The Great House [53] are architects of historic edifices, while the fathers of Adam of the Road [206] and Away Is So Far [81] earn their daily bread as strolling musicians but for widely divergent reasons. Adam's father has the true vocation and wanderlust of the minstrel, while Pedro's father is running blindly from his grief.

The two books, The Edge of Next Year [80] and Heads You Win; Tails I Lose [120], depict alcoholism in the middle and upper classes. In the former, Orin's father finds solace in a bottle on the death of his wife, and in the latter, Melissa's mother becomes inebriate when her husband leaves her. Orin finds a solution for rehabilitating his father, but Melissa is counseled that there is no cure and she must learn to cope with it until she is old enough to leave home.

The heroines of Listen to the Fig Tree [63] and A Dance to Still Music [106] have the handicaps of blindness and deafness, respectively, but learn to compensate so that they are not incapacitated; indeed, Muffin of Listen has even learned to use a sewing machine! Margaret of A Dance runs away from home when her mother remarries and finds succor with an unusual and independent woman, as does Stacy of Shelter from the Wind [98] upon her father's remarriage. Stacy eventually chooses to return home, but Margaret arranges to stay on with her benefactress. Court-appointed foster mothers head households in Ann Aurelia and Dorothy [190] and Who Cares About Espie Sanchez? [110], both of which have minority elements.

Mental problems are the common denominator of several titles. The Winds of Time [193] and Give Dad My Best [192] qualify as single-parent families because both mothers are in mental institutions. Mental retardation is a theme of Summer of the Swans [11], A Racecourse for Andy [214], and Dark Dreams [198].

Closely related are emotional problems. The Boy Who Could Make Himself Disappear [138] suffers psychosis as a result of his parents' egomaniacal machinations, and Florence of Growing Anyway Up [55] develops neurotic insularity after her father's death. Ellen Grae [103] and Samantha of Sam, Bangs and Moonshine [67] share a penchant for prevarication but for unrelated reasons. Ellen Grae fabricates for shock value, but Sam does so to compensate for the loss of her mother.

The protagonists of several books are rebellious or delinquent, including Andries [178], Big Blue Island [164], Chloris and the Creeps [139], J. T. [148], Love Is a Missing Person [122], My Brother Stevie [20], Queenie Peavy [189], That Jud! [154], There Is a Tide [6], Tough Chauncey [143], and Who Cares About Espie Sanchez [110]. Trouble on Treat Street [151] and Magdalena [174] explore mutual mistrust between members of different cultures, amicably reconciled. J. T. and Me Day [127] illustrate the father-absent phenomenon of the black ghetto for young readers.

It was concluded that bibliotherapy abounds, some of it in the form of synthetic "problem" or "formula books," others so mellifluously wrought that melancholy is dispelled in aesthetic victory. Realism is rank, much of it existing as steadfast, unpretentious, uncontroversial adventure. There is moralism and idealism, to be sure, in both periods, whether finely or coarsely crafted, but the strength and integrity of the fabric of the single-parent family in children's fiction is attributable to the variety and character of its warp and woof, affording librarians and others an abundant selection from satin to sacking, from serge to synthetics.

The Summary

By the analysis of the content of 215 books from preschool through junior high school portraying single parenthood (i.e., one adult acting in the capacity of parent or guardian to one or more children under 18 years of age) in children's literature from 1880 to 1976, it became apparent that contemporary authors are in fact keeping pace with social trends and demonstrating concern for the emotional crises of their intended readership, many of which crises are spawned by traumatic

Conclusions

disruptions in family structure. Given the diversity and individuality of the body of literature, a necessarily subjective way was devised to measure as accurately as possible the differences and similarities between existing examples of single parenthood in children's fiction published in or before 1965 and that published subsequently.

Because the distribution of the total of the 215 works placed 41 percent in the pre-1966 era and 59 percent in the subsequent decade, any similar distribution found in any of the categories of the evaluative criteria would indicate there was no significant variation between the two periods. Thus the representation of middle-class and suburban families was roughly commensurate for both periods, as was the absence of poverty. Also, proportionate number of authors chose to portray the missing parent(s) sympathetically and the condition of single parenthood as the secondary conflict in both periods. Twelve was the most frequently recorded age for the protagonists.

Areas which demonstrated the most striking gains (garnering 75 percent or more of the post-1966 totals) were the number of preschool/primary titles depicting single parenthood, the incidence of realism and bibliotherapeutic usefulness, and the number of titles given contemporary and urban settings. Black, Latin American, and lower-class manifestation showed remarkable increase, if still disproportionate to the total population. The portrayal of divorce/desertion/separation also moved beyond the earlier restrictive bounds with an almost commensurate number of new titles with authors plucky enough to depict the missing parent disparagingly. Use of the first-person idiom escalated, as did the depiction of single parenthood as the cause of primary conflict. Difficult adjustment on the child's part to a parent's remarriage gained significant representation in the more recent period.

Categories in which the pre-1966 period predominated with 55 percent or more of the totals were the number of Newbery medalists, the incidence of idealism and moralism, plus the ranks of titles that were neither moralistic nor bibliotherapeutic. The early period also commanded the greater percentage of historical fiction and period pieces (this last artificially inflated, as all pre-1960 books were arbitrarily made "period") and those that were set outside the United States and in a rural ambience. Widowhood prevailed prior to 1966, but widowed fathers outnumbered widowed mothers during that time by a slim but significant 8 percent. Orphan stories also held sway before 1966, but as with widowers, decisively more related and unrelated males headed households in the early period. The absent parent was more likely to be discreetly not mentioned before 1966; similarly, there were in that period fewer books showing the fact of single parenthood to be a cause of conflict.

The general assessment of poverty was inconclusive, but close analysis revealed a higher incidence of female and minority female (than male and minority male) poverty in both periods.

The paucity of preschool/primary books with a single-parent theme precluded any substantive judgment about the genre and seems to indicate that authors were cautious of controversy when writing for the very young. The need is especially apparent for a sensitive book portraying the death of a parent and more realistic titles in which the father is the single parent for young readers. It is time for Ms. Lexau to rise to another challenge.

Not all that was realistic was also bibliotherapeutic, as was seen, and not all that was bibliotherapeutic was also literary, but literariness will be left to another investigator to determine.

Part IV

EVALUATIVE CRITERIA
WITH CODING CHART FOR ALL 215 BOOKS

The following criteria were applied to each book; a comprehensive chart of the results appears on the following pages. Each left-hand page lists the books by entry number in the Annotated Bibliography. The succeeding columns relate directly to the following outline.

I. General Aspects

A Date of Publication
  1 Pre-1966
  2 Post-1966
B Audience
  1 Preschool/primary
  2 Intermediate
  3 Junior high
C Major Awards
  1 Newbery
  2 Caldecott

II. Genre

A Verisimilitude
  1 Realism
  2 Idealism
  3 Fantasy
B Message (may be more than one)
  1 Moralism
  2 Bibliotherapy
C Period
  1 Contemporary
  2 Historical fiction
  3 Period piece

III. Setting and Environment (may be more than one)

A Country
  1 U.S.
  2 Other
  3 Indeterminable
B Location
  1 Urban
  2 Suburban/small town
  3 Rural
  4 Indeterminable
C Milieu
  1 Upper class
  2 Middle class
  3 Lower class
  4 Not applicable
D Ethnic minority (U.S. only)
  1 Black
  2 Latin American
  3 Other

IV. Characterization

A Reason for single parenthood (may be more than one)
  1 Widowhood
  2 Divorce/desertion/separation
  3 Orphan with single guardian
  4 Protracted absence of parent(s)
  5 Other/indeterminable
B Single parent is (may be more than one)
  1 Mother
  2 Father
  3 Related female
  4 Related male
  5 Unrelated female
  6 Unrelated male
C Absent Parent is portrayed
  1 Sympathetically
  2 Unsympathetically
  3 Neutrally
  4 Not mentioned/indeterminable
D Poverty is a concern
  1 Yes
  2 No

V. Style and Plot

A Viewpoint
  1 First person
  2 Third person
B Single parenthood is source of
  1 Primary conflict
  2 Secondary conflict
  3 Insignificant conflict
C Change in family structure
  1 Remarriage/reconciliation
  2 Not applicable
D Adjustment to restructuring
  1 Relatively easy
  2 Relatively difficult

	I.A.		B.			C.			II.A.			B.			C.			III.A.			B.			C.				D.
	1	2	1	2	3	1	2	1	2	3	1	2	1	2	3	1	2	3	1	2	3	1	2	3	4	1	2	3	4	1
1		69	x						x					x			1			x			x			
2	64		x				x					x			x		1		x	x			x			
3		71	x			x						x		x					x					x		
4	47		x				x				x						2		x					x		
5		76		x			x		x	x							3			x		x			
6	64			x		x			x	x		x					x			x	x		x			
7	39		x			x					x		x				x			x			x			
8		72	x			x			x					x	x		x						x			
9	38		x			x	x		x			4		x			x			x		
10	80		x			x	x		x			1	x			x			
11		70		x	x	x		x	x		x			x		x	
12		71	x		x		x	x		x			x		x	
13	58	x		x		x		2	x			x
14	53		x	x		x	x		x		x	x
15	61		x	x		x	x		x		x
16		70	x	x		1	x		x
17		70	x	x	x	x	x	x		x
18		70	x	x	x	x	x	x		x
19		71	x	x	x	x	x		x
20		67	x	x	x	x	x	x
21		74	x	x	x	x x	x	x	x
22	65	x	x	x x	x	x
23		70	x	x	x	1	x	x
24		69	x	x	x x	x	x	x
25		75	x	x	x	1	x	x
26	54	x	x x	x x	x x	x
27	55	x	x x x	x x	x	x
28	52	x	x	x x	x x	x
29		75	x	x	x	x x	x	x
30		74	x	x	x	x	x	x
31		74	x	x	x	x	x	x x	x
32	43	x	x	x	x x	x	x
33	41	x	x	x x	x	x
34	42	x	x	x	x x	x	x
35	44	x	x	x	x x	x
36	51	x	x	x	x x	x	x
37	41	x	x	x x	x x
38	42	x	x	x x	x	x
39	43	x	x	x	x	x	x
40	62	x	x	x x	x	x
41		75	x	x	x	x	x	x	x
42		74	x	x	x	x	x	x	x
43		76	x	x	x	x	x	x
44		69	x	x	x x	x x	x	x	x	x
45		73	x	x	x	x x	x	x	x
46	51	x	x	x	5	x	x
47		66	x	x	x	1	x	x	x
48	64	x	x x	x	x	x
49	33	x	x	x	x	x
50	64	x	x	x	x	x

1. England
2. France
3. Wales
4. Denmark
5. Greenland

Evaluative Criteria 39

	IV. A.					B.						C.				D.	V. A.		B.		C.		D.	
2	3	1	2	3	4	5	1	2	3	4	5	6	1	2	3	4	1	2	1	2	1	2	3	1	2	1	2

(table of x marks — see original)

1. Aunt
2. Grandmother
3. Jewish-American
4. Irish-American
5. Uncle

The Single-Parent Family

	I. A.		B.			C.			II. A.			B.			C.			III. A.			B.				C.				D.
	1	2	1	2	3	1	2	1	2	3	1	2	1	2	3	1	2	3	1	2	3	4	1	2	3	4	1
51	64			x			x			x			x			x			x			x			
52		74	x			x			x	x		x		1	x			x			x			x	x
53	49			x			x				x		1			x			x						
54	01		x			x	x		x	x		x				x			x						
55		76		x		x		x	x			x				x			x						
56		66		x	x	x			x		x	x					x		x						
57		72		x		x		x		x			2		x			x							
58	59		x			x			x	x		x				x			x						
59	63			x		x			x	x		x			x			x							
60	55		x				x		x	x		x			x			x							
61	32		x	x		x						x		3	x				x						
62		75	x			x			x	x		x			x			x							
63		74		x		x			x	x		x			x						x	x			
64	34		x			x	x			x		x				x			x						
65	25		x			x	x					x	x			x			x						x
66	58		x			x						x	x		x			x							
67		66	x		x	x		x	x	x					x	x			x						
68	63		x				x					x	x			x		x	x	x					
69		75	x				x					x	x			x		x	x	x					
70	62		x		x				x		4		x			x									
71	40		x			x			x	x					x			x							
72	34		x	x		x			x		5	x				x									
73	80		x			x	x		x	x		x				x									
74		68	x			x		x	x		x			x			x								x
75	40		x	x		x		x	x		x		6	x	x										
76	55		x			x			x	x					x	x									
77	54		x		x		x		x	x					x		x								
78	63		x		x			x	x						x		x								
79		74	x		x		x		x					x		x									
80		74	x		x	x	x		x					x		x									
81		74	x		x	x	x			7		x		x											
82		74	x		x	x		x	x			x		x		x									
83		75	x		x	x	x	x		8	x		x												
84	54		x		x		x			8	x		x												
85	49		x		x		x	x		x			x												
86		69	x		x	x	x		x		x	x				x			x		x				
87		75	x		x	x	x	9	x	x	x														
88	63		x		x	x	x	x		x		x		x											
89	43		x		x	x	x	x	x		x		x												
90	48		x		x	x	x	x	x		x		x												
91		75	x		x	x	x	10	x			x													
92		71	x	x	x	x	x	x		x	x														
93	63		x		x	x	x		x	x															
94		69	x	x	x	x	x		x	x	x														
95	64		x	x	x	x	x	7	x	x															
96		75	x	x	x	x	x		x	x															
97		67	x	x	x	x	x	x	x	x															
98		76	x	x	x	x	x	x	x	x															
99		68	x	x	x	x	x	x																	
100		72	x	x	x	x	x	x	x																

1. England
2. Scotland
3. China
4. Denmark
5. Bulgaria
6. Polynesia
7. Spain
8. Switzerland
9. Russia
10. Angola

Evaluative Criteria 41

2	3	IV.A.1	2	3	4	5	B.1	2	3	4	5	6	C.1	2	3	4	D.1	V.A.2	1	B.2	1	2	C.3	1	D.2	1	2
		x					x						x					x	x		x		x		x		
		x					x						x				x		x	x				x			
		x						x							x		x	x				x		x			
		x					x							x		x		x		x				x			
		x					x							x			x	x	x				x				x
		x		x			x	1					x					x	x	x			x				x
		x					x						x				x			x	x				x		
		x						x					x						x	x		x		x			
		x						x					x				x		x		x		x	x			
		x					x								x	x			x				x	x		
		x					x						x				x		x				x	x		
x		x	x		x		x							x		x	x		x				x	x		
		x					x						x			x		x	x			x			
		x					x						x	x		x				x	x	
	2	x					x						x	x		x		x	x	x	
		x		x			x		x				x		x		x		x	
		x						x					x		x	x	x		x	
		x				x	x						x	x	x		x	x	
		x					x						x	x	x	x	x	x		x
		x					x						x	x	x	x	x	
		x				x				x			x	x	x	x	
		x				x				x			x	x	x	x	x	
		x				x				x	x	x	x	x	x	
	3	x			x	x	4			x		x	x	x	x	x	x
		x				x			x		x	x	x	x	x	x
		x				x			x	x	x	x	x	x	x
		x				x	x		x	x	x	x	x
		x				x	x		x	x	x	x	x
		x				x	x		x	x	x	x	x
		x				x	x		x	x	x	x	x
		x				x	x		x	x	x	x	x
		x	x	x		x	x	x	x	x	x
		x	x	x	x	x	x	x	x	x
		x	x	x	x	x	x	x	x
		x	x	x	x	x	x	x	x
		x	x	x	x	x	x	x	x
		x	x	x	x	x	x	x	x
		x	x	x	x	x x	x	x
		x	x	x	x	x	x	x	x
		x	x	x	x	x	x	x
		x	x	x	x	x	x
		x	x	x	x x	x
.	x	x	x	x	x x	x
x	x	x	x	x	x	x	x
x	x	x	x	x x	x	x
x	x	x	x	x	x	x
x	x	x	x	x x	x
x	x	x	x	x x	x
x	x	x	x	x	x x	x	x
x	x	x	x	x

1. Aunt
2. American Indian
3. Chinese-American
4. Grandmother

	I.A.2	I.B.1	I.B.2	I.B.3	I.C.1	I.C.2	II.A.1	II.A.2	II.A.3	II.B.1	II.C.1	II.C.2	II.C.3	III.A.1	III.A.2	III.A.3	III.B.1	III.B.2	III.B.3	III.B.4	III.C.1	III.C.2	III.C.3	III.C.4	D.1
101	72	x					x				x	x		x				x				x			
102	75	x						x			x	x		x					x		x				
103	67	x					x				x	x		x				x				x			
104	68	x					x					x		x				x			x	x			
105	76		x				x				x		x	x				x				x			
106	74	x					x				x	x		x				x					x		
107	71	x						x			x	x		x				x			x				
108	69	x					x				x	x		x			x					x			
109	71	x					x				x	x		x				x				x			
110	75	x						x			x	x		x			x						x		
111	75	x					x				x	x		x				x				x			
112	64		x				x			x	x	x		x				x			x				
113	65	x					x				x	x		x					x		x				
114	67	x					x					x		x				x						x	x
115	70		x				x				x	x		x				x				x			
116	69	x					x				x	x			x			x				x			
117	69	x					x				x	x		x			x					x			
118	75	x						x			x	x		x			x					x			
119	75	x					x					x		x			x					x			
120	73		x				x				x	x		x				x			x				
121	64		x				x					x		x					x		x				
122	75		x				x				x	x		x				x			x				x
123	73		x					x			x	x		x				x				x			
124	74	x					x				x	x		x				x	x			x			
125	75		x				x				x	x		x			x					x			
126	72	x					x				x	x		x				x				x			
127	71	x					x				x	x		x			x						x		x
128	76	x					x				x	x		x				x				x			
129	73		x				x				x	x		x			x					x			
130	71			x			x				x	x		x			x					x			
131	75			x			x				x	x		x			x						x		x
132	75	x					x				x	x		x						x		x			
133	68		x				x				x			x	1		x					x			
134	72			x			x				x	x		x				x					x		
135	75	x					x				x	x		x				x		x					
136	74		x					x			x	x		x				x				x			
137	75		x					x			x	x		x				x				x			
138	68		x				x				x	x		x			x				x				
139	73	x					x				x	x		x				x				x			
140	75		x				x				x	x		x				x				x			
141	71	x					x				x	x		x			x						x		
142	75	x					x				x	x		x				x				x			
143	74		x				x				x	x		x				x				x			
144	75		x				x				x	x		x				x				x			
145	68		x			x	x	x			x			x		x					x				
146	72		x				x				x	x		x				x				x			
147	76	x				x					x	x		x				x				x			x
148	69	x					x				x	x		x			x						x		x
149	76		x				x				x	x		x			x					x			
150	71	x				x					x	x				x				x		x			

1. Sweden

Evaluative Criteria

2	3	IV. A. 1	2	3	4	5	B. 1	2	3	4	5	6	C. 1	2	3	4	D. 1	V. A. 2	1	B. 2	1	2	C. 3	1	2	D. 1	2
		x					x							x				x	x		x				x		
		x					x								x			x		x	x				x		
		x						x					x					x	x				x		x		
		x						x					x					x	x				x		x		
		x					x						x						x		x		x		x		
		x					x								x		x		x		x		x				x
	1	x	x				x		2				x					x	x		x				x		
		x					x		2							x		x	x		x				x		
		x					x						x					x		x	x			x			x
x		x					x				x			x	x				x	x				x			
		x					x						x					x		x	x			x			x
		x					x						x					x		x	x			x			x
		x	x				x		2					x				x		x	x			x		x	
		x	x				x								x	x			x	x				x			
		x					x	x						x				x	x			x			x		x
		x					x								x			x		x	x				x		
		x					x								x			x	x		x				x		
		x					x						x					x	x		x				x	x	
		x					x								x			x	x		x				x		
		x					x							x				x	x			x			x		
		x					x								x			x		x	x				x		
		x					x								x			x	x			x		x			x
		x					x						x					x	x		x			x		x	
		x					x	x					x					x	x		x				x		
	3	x					x						x					x	x		x			x		x	
		x					x								x			x		x	x				x		
		x						x					x				x			x	x				x		
		x						x					x					x			x	x			x		
		x						x					x					x	x		x				x		
		x						x	x				x						x	x	x			x			x
		x					x							x		x		x	x						x		
		x					x						x						x	x	x				x		
		x					x							x		x		x	x	x			x				x
		x					x								x	x	x		x			x		x			
		x						x					x					x	x		x				x		x
		x					x								x			x		x		x		x			
		x						x						x				x		x		x		x		x	
		x					x							x				x		x			x		x		
x		x					x								x			x	x				x	x			x
x		x					x						x					x	x		x				x		
		x					x							x			x		x		x				x		
		x					x						x					x	x		x			x			x
		x					x							x				x		x	x				x		
		x					x							x				x		x		x			x		
		x				x									x		x		x				x		x		
		x					x						x					x		x	x			x			x
		x					x						x					x		x		x		x			x
		x					x							x			x			x		x			x		
		x					x						x					x	x		x				x		x
		x					x									x		x	x		x				x		

1. American Indian
2. Grandmother
3. Vietnamese-American

44   The Single-Parent Family

	I. A. 1	2	B. 1	2	3	C. 1	2	II. A. 1	2	3	B. 1	2	C. 1	2	3	III. A. 1	2	3	B. 1	2	3	4	C. 1	2	3	4	D. 1
151	74	x						x				x	x				x			x						x		x
152	66			x					x				x					1			x					x		
153	75	x								x			x				x			x					x			
154	57		x					x				x			x	x				x				x				
155	66	x						x				x		x	x					x				x				
156	64	x						x				x	x				x				x				x			
157	11	x							x		x	x			x			2			x		x					
158	74	x						x				x	x				x			x				x				
159	52	x		x				x							x			3			x		x					
160	69	x						x				x	x				x				x				x			
161	65	x						x			x		x						x	x				x				
162	66	x							x			x		x	x					x				x				
163	68	x							x					x	x			x						x				
164	64	x						x				x	x				x			x					x			
165	62	x								x		x			x					x				x				
166	56	x						x		x				x	x					x				x				
167	48	x						x						x	x					x				x				
168	64		x					x			x	x			x			x							x		x
169	70	x						x			x	x			x			x							x		x
170	60		x						x					x		4			x				x				
171	38			x				x			x	x		x	x					x					x		x
172	76	x						x				x		x	x					x				x			
173	58			x				x		x			x	x						x	x			x				
174	71	x						x			x	x			x			x							x			
175	80		x					x		x			x		5				x				x				
176	64		x					x			x				2	x							x				
177	74	x						x		x	x		x			x			x							
178	42		x					x	x			x			6		x			x					
179	66	x						x		x	x		x					x				x			
180	63		x				x				x	x		x					x				x				
181	60		x					x			x				4		x				x				
182	62		x					x			x				4		x				x				
183	49		x					x	x		x		x			x						x			
184	38		x					x				x	x	7		x					x				
185	69	x		x	x					x	x		x				x				x		x
186	63		x					x			x			2		x				x				
187	53			x		x				x		x		8		x				x				
188	64		x				x		x	x				9		x						x	
189	66	x				x				x	x		x			x					x			
190	68	x				x		x	x	x		x			x				x		x
191	47		x			x			x		x	x			x				x		
192	76		x			x			x		x	x		x				x		
193	74		x			x		x		x				x	x			
194	67	x				x		x			2		x			x		
195	70	x				x	x	x			8		x			x		
196	62		x	x		x	x x		x		2		x			x		
197	31			x	x				x		2		x			x		
198	74	x		x		x x		x		x				x		
199	70	x		x		x x			x	x					x	
200	66	x		x			x	10		x				x	

1. Scotland   2. England
3. Peru   4. Sweden
5. Switzerland   6. Holland
7. Italy   8. Germany
9. Ethiopia   10. Hungary

Evaluative Criteria   45

IV.A.2	3	1	2	3	B.4	5	1	2	.3	4	C.5	6	1	2	3	4	D.1	V.A.2	1	B.2	1	2	C.3	1	D.2	1	2
x			x					1				x					x		x	x					x		
			x							x							x	x	x	x					x		
			x					2								x	x	x	x			x		x		
			x							x	x						x	x	x			x		x		
			x								x				x		x	x	x	x				x		
			x						x					x			x	x	x	x				x		
		x	x			x		2			x						x	x	x			x		x		
			x					3						x			x	x	x			x		x		
			x						x	x							x	x	x					x		
		x	x			x	4			x			x	x			x	x			x			x		
			x							x	x			x		x		x						x		
			x				2			x				x	x	x			x					
			x					x		x			x		x	x		x		x		x	
6			x				5				x		x		x	x	x		x			x		
6			x				3						x	x		x	x					x		
			x			1							x		x			x		x			
			x			2							x	x		x			x		x			
			x			1							x	x		x			x		x			
			x			1				x				x	x		x	x					x		
			x			7		x					x		x	x					x		
6			x			8		x				x		x		x					x		
			x			2				x		x	x				x		x			
x	x		x		x	1					x	x	x			x		x			
			x			3					x	x	x		x			x		x			
			x				x				x	x		x	x					x		
			x			8			x			x	x	x					x		
			x			2		x			x	x	x		x		x		x	
			x			1			x			x				x		x			
			x				x			x	x		x		x			x		
				x		8		x				x	x		x		x			
				x		8		x				x	x		x		x			
9				x				x				x	x		x		x			
				x	x			x				x	x		x	x		x			
				x	x			x		x		x	x	x		x			
				x	x	8		x				x		x		x			
				x	x			x				x		x		x			
				x	x			x				x	x	x		x			
				x	x			x	x		x		x	x		x			
				x	x		x		x			x		x	x	x	x		x
				x	x			x			x		x	x		x			
				x	x				x	x	x			x		x			
			x							x		x	x		x			
			x	x				x			x	x	x		x			
			x		1			x			x	x		x		x			
			x	x				x			x	x	x		x			
			x	x				x			x	x		x	x			
9	x		x		x	1		x			x	x	x		x			
x			x	x				x			x		x	x		x			
			x	x				x				x		x	x		x			

1. Grandmother
2. Uncle
3. Grandfather
4. Sister
5. Great Uncle
6. American Indian
7. Great Grandmother
8. Aunt
9. Italian-American

	I. A.		B.		C.		II. A.			B.		C.			III. A.			B.			C.				D.
	1	2	1	2	3	1	2	1	2	3	1	2	1	2	3	1	2	3	1	2	3	4	1	2	3	4	1
201	45		x					x			x			x		x				x				x			
202		75			x			x						x		x			x						x		
203	53		x						x					x			x		x					x			
204		66	x						x		x	x					x		x					x			
205	44		x			x					x	x		x	x		x			x						x	
206	42		x		x	x								x		1 2				x				x			
207		68	x					x			x	x				x			x					x			
208		72	x					x			x	x		x			x		x					x			
209		70	x					x				x		x			x		x					x			
210	43		x			x			x						x		x					x	x	x			
211		69	x						x			x					x			x				x			
212	60			x		x					x			x							x			x			
213		75		x		x			x			x	x					x						x		x	x
214		68	x					x			x					3				x				x			
215		74	x					x			x	x					x			x				x			

1. England
2. Sweden
3. Australia

Evaluative Criteria

	IV.													V.								
	A.					B.							C.			D.	A.		B.		C.		D.
2	3	1	2	3	4	5	1	2	3	4	5	6	1	2	3	4	1	2	1	2	1	2	3	1	2	1	2

(table with x marks and numbers as shown)

1. Chinese-American
2. Indeterminable
3. Polish-American
4. Unwed Mother
5. Grandmother

Two books appear in incorrect classifications, not discovered until all the preceding statistical work was completed. Their inclusion in erroneous categories in no way affects the statistics or the validity of the conclusions drawn, however. Shotwell's Magdalena [174], whose father is a seaman, rightfully belongs under Protracted absence of parent(s), not Orphan with single guardian. Corcoran's The Winds of Time [193], which appears in the Protracted absence portion, should be in the Divorce/desertion/separation category.

V

ANNOTATED BIBLIOGRAPHY

WIDOWHOOD

1. Barber, Antonia. The Ghosts. New York: Farrar, Straus and Giroux, 1969. Grades 5-8.
    An elderly ghost from the 1800's returns to the present to make propitiation for a sin of omission in the past which resulted in the deaths of two innocent children. These children, ghosts themselves, appear to Lucy and Jamie and show them how to travel the Wheel of Time back to their day before the fatal fire. With the help of Jamie and Lucy, their hapless fate is averted and old Mr. Blunden's spirit makes expiation and is laid to rest. Back in the present after a harrowing transversal, it is miraculously discovered that Jamie and Lucy are the great-great-grandchildren of one of the ghost children (who lived happily to a ripe old age), and her country estate where they have been living as caretakers is legally theirs, bringing fresh bloom to the pallid countenance of their tragically widowed mother.

2. Bawden, Nina. Three on the Run. Philadelphia: J. B. Lippincott, 1964. Illus. by Wendy Worth. Grades 5-8.
    Ben Mallory, now 12 [see 186], comes to London to visit his father and discovers international intrigue. A sheltered African boy, son of an imprisoned prime minister, is being held in protective custody by his two uncles in the house just beyond the garden wall. When Ben overhears one of the uncles plotting to kidnap the boy and force a political coup against his father, he helps Thomas escape, and along with Lil, a Cockney waif only one step ahead of welfare because her mother is hospitalized, they stow away aboard a dray destined for Ben's seaside hometown where they take refuge in

a cave on the beach. The wicked uncle and his henchman eventually track them and stalk them from the beach and cliff in a chilling climax. When they are finally caught, Ben's aunt causes enough of a delaying action that the coup fizzles before the uncle can spirit Thomas away. The fathers are reunited with their sons and bring with them Lil's mother to recuperate in the wholesome sea air at Aunt Mabel's.

3. Beckett, Hilary. <u>My Brother Angel</u>. New York: Dodd, Mead, 1971. Illus. by Louis Glanzman. Grades 4-6.

Carlos, 13, has the gift of <u>telepatía</u> or second sight which enables him to sense his grandmother's illness in distant Texas. When his mother rushes to her side, Carlos is left in charge of his little brother Angel, 5, in their shabby but respectable home in New York City. A series of thefts and other disturbances in the neighborhood culminates in an eerie Halloween outing in which Carlos' <u>telepatía</u> warns him of impending danger to Angel. Angel, however, has already subdued the miscreant, who stole to feed his drug habit, and released the addict's young sister from her psychological dependence on him. Angel's cat Gato is a major catalyst of the story, and elements of Mexican-American heritage and ethnic discrimination are important adjuncts.

4. Bishop, Claire Hutchet. <u>Pancakes-Paris</u>. New York: Viking Press, 1947. Illus. by Georges Schreiber. Grades 3-5.

Post-World War II Paris in February is anything but gay for its denizens. Homes are cold, people are hungry, and there are dire shortages of the most basic necessities. Ten-year-old Charles remembers prewar days before his father's imprisonment in Germany and subsequent death when they had traditional crepes for Mardi Gras, but his 5-year-old sister does not believe such amplitude. Two American soldiers give him a box of Aunt Jemima pancake mix in return for a favor, but alas, he cannot read the English directions. A friendly lady at the American Embassy translates them, and he starts preparing them as a surprise for his mother and sister until he realizes he has nothing with which to grease the griddle. The soldiers appear suddenly with powdered milk and eggs, butter, syrup, cocoa, candy, and precious soap, and they all celebrate an old-fashioned Mardi Gras.

Bibliography

5. Bond, Nancy. A String in the Harp. New York: Atheneum, 1976. Grades 7-10.

    Following his wife's tragic death in an auto accident, David Morgan, English professor at Amherst, accepts a teaching position at a remote university in Wales to try to escape his grief, taking with him his two younger children, Peter, 12, and Becky, 10, leaving 15-year-old Jen at home with relatives to finish high school. Jen joins the family at Christmas and discovers tension and irritation dividing them. Peter is spiteful and truculent at being torn from friends and familiar foundations and transplanted to the desolation of the Welsh seacoast, while Dad has severed communications by his absorption in his work. Then Peter finds an ancient artifact that makes him yet more aloof and peculiar. It is a magical singing harp key that conjures trancelike visions of the legendary bard Taliesin, embroiling the family and their friends in a sixth-century adventure. When an impersonal museum director asks Peter to relinquish the relic, Peter knows he must restore it to its rightful owner, and sets about to find Taliesin's final resting place. Having learned so much of Welsh history and accomplished his mission, Peter is sympathetic to Wales, and with trust restored, the entire family decides to stay another year.

6. Bragdon, Elspeth. There Is a Tide. New York: Viking Press, 1964. Illus. by Lilian Obligado. Grades 6-9.

    As 15-year-old Nat is about to be expelled from yet another of the succession of private boarding schools his pedantic, punctilious father has consigned him to, the perceptive headmaster suggests that father and son make a pilgrimage to the school's retreat on an island off the coast of Maine to get acquainted with one another, the crux of the rebellious boy's problem. Nat loves the old house on sight but is less enthusiastic about the taciturn islanders until he makes an honest effort to understand and appreciate their distinctive quality and earn their respect and acceptance. While Nat is groping and growing, his father seems impervious to the rest-cure, continuing to work in aloof condescension until the death of a peculiar old man, grandfather of the elusive orphan Sue. A brief spate of recollection and confession, like the click of a shutter, reveals a glimpse of his father's emotions and signals optimism for the development of a normal relationship.

7. Brink, Carol Ryrie. Winter Cottage. New York: Macmillan, 1939. Illus. by Fermin Rocker. Grades 5-6.
When his grocery business fails at the beginning of the Great Depression, Pop, an improvident but eloquent poetry quoter, loads his unsold inventory into the trailer and his daughters Araminta, 13, and Eglantine, 10, into the battered auto and departs for Aunt Amy's grudging charity. The car breaks down in the Wisconsin woods near a summer cottage closed for the winter. Lacking funds to repair the car, they elect to spend the winter at the cozy former farmhouse where a runaway boy joins them. Minty, the pragmatic one of the family, attempts to extract Pop's secret recipe for his stupendous pancakes, sockdollagers, gollwhollickers, and whales, to enter in a flour company contest and win the prize to pay rent for the cottage, abetted by her sister Eggs and Joe, the runaway. Unexpected visitors arriving in a blizzard arouse mutual suspicion, but Pop's friendly hospitality palliates it. Minty's suspected Chicago gangsters are nothing more than the cottage's rightful owners who soon abandon their design to have the interlopers arrested. Minty's check comes through in the spring with enough left over after rent for Pop to open his long dreamed-of secondhand bookstore.

8. Bulla, Clyde Robert. Open the Door and See All the People. New York: Thomas Y. Crowell, 1972. Illus. by Wendy Watson. Grades 3-5.
When their rented farmhouse burns to the ground, JoAnn, 7, and Teeney, 6, can save nothing, not even their dolls. With money from the sale of the cow, their mother decides to move to the city where an old friend finds them modest lodgings and Mamma a job as a chambermaid. They have nothing left over for frills, but Teeney is miserable without her doll until a neighbor girl tells them of the magical Toy House where dolls can be borrowed for two weeks like library books and can even be adopted permanently if the little girls prove their solicitude. JoAnn and Teeney are model mothers for the six-week probationary period until the day before the formal adoption ceremony when the neighbor's dog kidnaps Teeney's Baby and licks its face off. The kindly Doll Man solves the problem and even Mamma gets the doll she never had.

9. Burglon, Nora. Sticks Across the Chimney. New York: Holiday Hse., 1938. Illus. by F. Eichenberg. Grades 4-6.
Storks nesting on their chimney is a talisman of

good fortune for Siri, Erik, and their mother when they come to live at Gravsted farm, which the superstitious villagers claim is haunted by a malevolent Viking spirit. But the diligent and enterprising family and their pet duck, King Christian the Builder, brave adherents of the tenet that "generosity begets good," foil the vexatious villagers by prospering in the teeth of adversity. The arrival of their eccentric grandfather, an archaeologist, precipitates action, adventure, and the discovery of ancient treasures in the grave mound, concluding with the establishment of a thriving cottage industry and a visit from royalty. A generous smorgasbord of Danish history and heritage is also spread.

10. Burnett, Frances Hodgson. <u>A Little Princess.</u> New York: Platt and Munk, 1967 (c1892). Illus. by Stewart Sherwood. Grades 5-6.
    Captain Crewe settles his 7-year-old pampered but unspoiled darling Sara in luxury at Miss Minchin's Select Seminary for Young Ladies in London and returns to his regiment in India. Isolated by the jealousy of schoolmates and Miss Minchin alike, the lonely girl befriends the school dunce, mothers the youngest pupil, patronizes the scullary maid Becky, and earns their adoration. Word comes that her father had made his fortune in diamond mines but has lost it and his life just as quickly. The princess-turned-pauper is promptly relegated to the attic with Becky where she tames the rats for companionship. The vulgar, avaricious Miss Minchin starves her, freezes her, and works her to exhaustion, but breeding tells and her pride and bearing never falter. When her fortune is belatedly restored by the enigmatic Indian gentleman next door, she is not vindictive but sends for Becky to be her handmaiden.

11. Byars, Betsy. <u>The Summer of the Swans.</u> New York: Viking Press, 1970. Illus. by Ted CoConis. Grades 5-7.
    At 15 Sara is feeling very ambivalent and self-conscious about her appearance and her 10-year-old brother who has been mentally retarded since a serious illness in infancy. Her older sister Wanda, 19, is popular, attractive, and well-adjusted with no problem more serious than cajoling Aunt Willie, their guardian, to loosen the apron strings. When their mother died six years ago their father lost interest in the family except for support payments. One day Sara takes Charlie

to see swans that are visiting at a nearby lake. They make such an impression on him that he wanders off in the middle of the night to try to see them again. In Sara's desperation to find him she learns that the boy she believes to be her enemy is really a stalwart friend. She also realizes that everyone has obstacles of one magnitude or another to contend with and moping over them is non-constructive.

12. Cameron, Eleanor. A Room Made of Windows. Boston: Little, Brown, 1971. Illus. by Trina Schart Hyman. Grades 7-9.

   Adolescent Julia shares with her dead father the burning compulsion to write. She follows her vocation at the desk he made for her in her private sanctuary and window on the world. Her endeavors are encouraged by her new friend, an elderly neighbor who is an accomplished musician and kindred spirit. When her mother reveals her plans to marry an old family friend, Julia reacts negatively in rage and rebellion, burnishing her father's tarnished image and succeeding in distressing her mother and older brother. One of her fears is that of leaving her beloved room and neighborhood friends near San Francisco, but it is assuaged when two of the friends leave first and she makes advance friends at the new home nearby. Julia is gradually shown that her selfishness and obstinacy benefit no one, not even herself.

13. Carlson, Natalie Savage. The Family Under the Bridge. New York: Harper, 1958. Illus. by Garth Williams. Grades 3-5.

   The jaunty old hobo Armand, who has an antipathy for both children and work, returns to his roost on the quay under one of Paris' famous bridges, only to find that his niche has been appropriated by three homeless, fatherless moppets. The little "starlings" suffer him to stay, although their mother is mistrustful of the disreputable beggar. The children quickly endear themselves to him, and he takes them to see Father Christmas, a friend seasonally employed at a fancy department store. They ask for nothing but a real home. When two officious society matrons threaten to send the children to an orphanage and their mother to jail, he hastily removes them to the camp of gypsy friends, to their mother's initial horror. When the gypsies move on, he is forced to consider gainful employment. Transformed by a bath and a mend, courtesy of the children's mother, he is engaged as concierge of an apartment house, the perfect sinecure because the emolument includes living quarters where he can nest his new brood.

14. Cavanna, Betty. Love, Laurie. Philadelphia: Westminster Press, 1953. Grades 7-9.

    Two months following her mother's death, 16-year-old Laurie and her father forsake the suburban house with its poignant memories and move into the old inn in town for the summer while they await completion of the new house on their country property near Philadelphia. On moving day, the socially immature girl meets Mike, the most attractive boy she's ever seen, and spends the summer worrying whether the feeling is mutual and being jealous of her vivacious best friend who has also set her cap for Mike. At the same time she is totally relaxed with the erudite young immigrant whom she regards as a platonic friend and is condescending to the stodgy son of her father's friend until both young men display a more than casual interest in her and she realizes that different boys have different qualities to offer. Because her father is absent on business most of the time, she is forced to make decorating decisions on the new house that her highly competent mother would normally have made and so gains confidence in other ways, too.

15. _____. A Touch of Magic. Philadelphia: Westminster Press, 1961. Illus. by John Gretzer. Grades 7-9.

    Quaker Hannah is 13 as the Declaration of Independence is being signed and gets a worm's-eye view of the Revolution from her mother's modest row house in Philadelphia as seamstress and sometime confidante to the aristocratic Shippen cousins and part-time spy for the ragtag Continental Army. She observes the opulence, gayety, and romantic intrigue of the British occupation, the star-crossed marriages of willful Peggy and winsome Nancy Shippen, and shares the deprivation and degradation of the victims of war through her agonizing involvement with her childhood sweetheart who is engaged in intelligence for Washington and is the scarred survivor of a pestilential prison camp. An epilogue set in 1804 contrasts her simple but serene marriage to those of the darling daughters of privilege whose lives once seemed touched by a magic that quickly tarnished.

16. Christopher, John. <u>The Prince in Waiting</u>. New York: Macmillan, 1970. Grades 6-9.

   In a future feudalistic society in which all technology is taboo and primitive armed city states are ruled by warrior princes manipulated by holy Seers who interpret the will of the omnipotent Spirits, ambitious 13-year-old Luke wrests the prized jeweled sword from his nobler companions in jousting contest and becomes a Young Captain and heir apparent to power when his father is acclaimed Prince. Their glory and good fortune are short-lived, however, when Luke's mother is killed by his father's jealous first wife who thinks her son should be his father's successor. Brutality, destruction, and treachery ensue in wars among the city states, and Luke is forced to flee for his life to the Sanctuary of the High Seers where he learns the awesome secret of the Seers and Spirits and the explanation behind the decimation of earth, the Burning Lands, and the defective Polymuf mutants.

17. Cleaver, Vera, and Bill Cleaver. <u>The Mimosa Tree</u>. Philadelphia: J. B. Lippincott, 1970. Grades 5-8.

   Following a feud with their backwoods neighbors during which their hogs sicken and die and their crops rot in the fields, the five Proffitt children, 4, 7, 9, 10, and 14, and their blind Pa are persuaded by their blowsy, vulgar stepmother to pull up stakes in rural North Carolina and move to a better life in Chicago. Their tenement is barren of any living thing, so 14-year-old Marvella invents a mimosa tree in the alley to placate Pa. Of more immediacy is the fact that the stepmother deserts them, leaving the naive hillbillies who have never heard of crime, drugs, welfare, or broken homes unprepared for survival in the slum jungle. Reared in the Christian work ethic, they look for jobs but are told it is illegal to hire children, yet bureaucratic indifference snarls financial assistance, and purse snatching becomes their sole means of livelihood. When the street urchin who taught them the trade pushes his mother in front of a bus, it shocks Marvella into realizing that returning home is the only way of regaining their dormant pride and integrity. The neighbors welcome them back warmly.

18. _____, and _____. <u>Grover</u>. Philadelphia: J. B. Lippincott, 1970. Illus. by Frederic Marvin. Grades 5-6.

   Eleven-year-old Grover's well-meaning family shield

him from the fact that his mother has cancer. Only his mother herself tries to prepare him in an oblique way for her eventual death by reminding him that he favors her side of the family which doesn't "howl" over eventualities. Soon afterward she calmly ends her life with a gun. His father suffers openly and refuses to acknowledge or condone her premature absence. Grover stoically pursues his daily rounds with friends Ellen Grae and Farrell, allowing his emotions to escape only once in clumsily decapitating a neighbor's turkey in anger, struggling to plumb the unfathomable depths of mortality. On a visit to her grave, Grover realizes that his father is sorry for himself, not her, and allows his mind to "turn a corner." A fish head in the chowder cracks his father's mask of grief just enough to admit the first glimmering of recovery.

19. ──────────, and ──────────. I Would Rather Be a Turnip. Philadelphia: J. B. Lippincott, 1971. Grades 5-7.

Ostracized by her erstwhile friends when her sister's illegitimate child comes to live with her and her pharmacist father in their small Southern town, 12-year-old Annie feels stultified and covered with contumely. Rebellion, revenge, and running away fail to restore her self-respect. Attempts at expressing herself in prose and poetry are unsatisfactory. A triumphant piano recital and her heroic rescue of her bright, studious nephew from a mad bull offer only temporary respite from her despondency. It is 8-year-old Calvin himself who introduces her to the world of literature and the knowledge it imparts. Words written by Helen Keller inspire her to look beyond "the fixity of limitations" through books. She discovers that William the Conqueror was illegitimate yet became king of England in spite of benighted bigots.

20. Clymer, Eleanor. My Brother Stevie. New York: Holt, Rinehart and Winston, 1967. Grades 4-6.

Annie, 10, and her younger brother Stevie, 8, were abandoned by their mother after their father's death and now live with their grandmother on welfare in a housing project in New York. Grandma can't control Stevie by her physical and verbal abuse, and Annie becomes increasingly worried over his delinquent behavior. A dedicated new teacher, wise and sympathetic Miss Stover, briefly reverses this trend by channeling his energy into constructive and meaningful activities, but when she is summoned home by a family emergency, Stevie drifts back to his old ways and unsavory companions. In desperation Annie seeks Miss Stover's address in the country and borrows money to buy train tickets for Stevie and her to make the round trip. An overnight visit in the pleasant bustle of the rural foster home that Miss Stover grew up in and now helps manage has a cleansing and uplifting influence on both children, and they return to the city with the promise and inspiration of future visits in that wholesome atmosphere where they are accepted and respected.

21. Cohen, Barbara. Thank You, Jackie Robinson. New York: Lothrop, Lee and Shepard, 1974. Illus. by Richard Cuffari. Grades 4-6.

   Ten-year-old Sam lives and breathes baseball, has memorized the record books, and roots for the Brooklyn Dodgers, but has never attended a game because his mother and three sisters do not share his enthusiasm. When the elderly black man, Davy, becomes chef at the inn Sam's mother manages singlehandedly since his father's death three years earlier, shy Sam finally finds a friend and boon companion. Davy is a Dodger fan in general and of Jackie Robinson in particular, and together they travel to as many games as time permits. When a heart attack puts Davy in the hospital, Sam courageously makes the pilgrimage to Ebbets Field alone to get a ball autographed for Davy. The ball isn't powerful enough medicine to save his friend, and Sam is inconsolable. He turns on the radio just as Jackie comes to bat and whispers, "Hit it for Davy," and is rewarded for his faith. Positive messages on race, religion and death.

22. Constant, Alberta Wilson. Those Miller Girls! New York: Thomas Y. Crowell, 1965. Illus. by Joe and Beth Krush. Grades 5-6.

   When Papa accepts the position of history professor at Eastern Kansas Classical College in 1909, Lou Emma, 12, and Maddy, 11, persuade him that they don't need a housekeeper but can manage on their own. Lou Emma, who takes most of the responsibility, wishes secretly, however, that Papa will remarry, and she has already picked out their stepmother, the attractive new milliner in town. Miss Kate saves the day when Papa forgets until the last minute about the de rigueur reception staged annually by the college president's wife, connives with the girls to keep a pet goat over Papa's objections, devises a scheme to make a telescope for the college so Papa can teach astronomy, and shares in family frolic, triumph and ignominy at the Chautauqua held by the river that summer. Logical Papa doesn't appreciate what an indispensable jewel Miss Kate is until his maiden sister visits, but he quickly amends past oversight, and Miss Kate gets a ready-made, not secondhand, family.

23. Cookson, Catherine. The Nipper. Indianapolis: Bobbs-Merrill, 1970. Illus. by Tessa Jordan. Grades 6-8.

Sixteen-year-old Sandy and his mother are evicted from their farm cottage in northeast England in 1830 and are obliged to move to the shanty of a derelict coal miner, Mad Mark. Ma finds field work, but Sandy takes a grueling job in the mine when he learns that his pony, the Nipper, has been sold to be a pit pony. The disgruntled miners are divided into two factions. The one led by gentle Tom Fitzsimmons is peaceable and wants to negotiate, but the one headed by cruel, underhanded Big Mullen is bellicose and violent. Their gang is intent on wresting the location of the secret tunnel to the manor house from Mad Mark by torture or guile. Sandy befriends the old miner and is led to the tunnel's destination. When Sandy learns of Big Mullen's plan to blow up the house and its occupants on the night of a grand soiree it is too late to stop him, but on the Nipper's fleet legs he arrives at the house just in time to avert disaster. In his gratitude Sir William grants him whatever he desires, and thus he wins negotiation rights for the miners, and his mother wins Tom Fitzsimmons.

24. Corcoran, Barbara. Sasha, My Friend. New York: Atheneum, 1969. Illus. by Richard L. Shell. Grades 7-9.

In the plane crash that claimed her mother's life, 15-year-old Hallie's father sustained lung damage, and on his doctor's advice they leave their amenable home, friends, and accoutrements of civilization in smoggy Los Angeles and move to a tiny trailer without plumbing or electricity on the Christmas tree farm in the Montana wilderness where her father grew up. Miles from the nearest settlement, their only neighbors are an old Indian and a frontier family with a vicious son and a crippled daughter who becomes Hallie's only friend. She tries with all her might to cope with the solitude, danger, inconvenience, and rawness of a wilderness winter without success until she finds the orphaned wolf cub, Sasha, who puts meaning back into her life. Sasha saves her life one day when she is attacked by a wounded lynx, but she is unable to save his when the spiteful neighbor boy sees him as a menace and lays a trap for him, plunging her back into despair. She reacts with plucky resolve, however, when her father contracts pneumonia on the eve of the Christmas tree harvest, and she discovers how supportive and interdependent the denizens of the northern woods must be. Boarding in the nearest town solves her correspondence school problem, and she will see her father on weekends.

25. Dahl, Roald. <u>Danny the Champion of the World.</u> New York: Alfred A. Knopf, 1975. Illus. by Jill Bennett. Grades 4-6.

Danny's mother died when he was an infant, and the boy was reared happily if somewhat unconventionally in a gypsy encampment behind his father's small country filling station and garage. Only when he is 9 does his father's peculiar penchant for poaching pheasants from the forest preserves of Squire Hazel surface, a hobby shared by the vicar, the doctor, and the constable. Each has his own method of snaring the prize fowl, and Danny is soon inducted into the intricacies of the sport. After rescuing his injured father from the gamekeeper's diabolical trap, Danny becomes the world champion poacher, employing his wit and a product of modern medical science, and hysterically spoiling choleric Mr. Hazel's posh annual turkeyshoot.

26. Daringer, Helen F. <u>Bigity Anne.</u> New York: Harcourt, Brace and World, 1954. Illus. by Don Sibley. Grades 5-6.

Father is off in the jungles of Ecuador engineering a road for his oil company; Mrs. Malet, the housekeeper, has been called away to care for her daughter; and Mrs. Lloyd, her shrewish replacement, has pushed the Todd children, 13, 10, 7, and 5, to the limit of their endurance. Thirteen-year-old Anne summarily dismisses her and takes on the task of caring for her brothers and sister alone. Mrs. Lloyd tries to get the last word, however, by firing off a deprecatory letter to the county judge who opens an investigation. He supports the children but suggests that they share chores to take some of the onus off Anne. His inquiry also discloses that the children's father is missing in the jungle, and there is the grave possibility that the fiercely loyal little family may have to be separated to go to distant relatives. Father's sudden reappearance saves them.

27. _____. Like a Lady. New York: Harcourt, Brace and World, 1955. Illus. by Susan Knight. Grades 6-8.

Johanna, 13, has been saving for years to buy a collie pup. No ordinary mutt will suffice, because when you are poor "and your mother has to work for a living, you need to have a dog that you and your mother and your sister (9) can be proud of." When Mother has a chance to be elected a delegate to represent Oak Corners at a state PTA conference, she generously decides to forgo her savings and earn more to buy her a decent dress to replace her shabby "made-over" skirt and blouse. Ignoring the derisive gibes of her more affluent but less popular classmates, she and her friends have fun on money-raising projects and befriend an old man. She fails to achieve her goal, but her mother is elected anyway on the strength of her character and ability, not appearance, and the grateful graybeard makes Jo a present of her favorite collie pup.

28. _____. Stepsister Sally. New York: Harcourt, Brace and World, 1952. Illus. by Garrett Price. Grades 6-8.

Salubrious Sally has lived all her young life since her mother's death in her grandmother's small-town home with infrequent visits from her father, a hardware dealer who remained in the city. Father has remarried and acquired a built-in family and now wants Sally to join them, uprooting her from her secure and complacent life with Gran. Sally combines the patience of Job with the wisdom of Solomon in eventually earning the acceptance of her fractious stepsister Dorothy without much assistance from her unintentionally vacuous, equivocating father. Her new brothers and stepmother are more sympathetically portrayed.

29. DeAngeli, Marguerite. The Lion in the Box. Garden City, N.Y.: Doubleday, 1975. Illus. by the author. Grades 3-5.

Papa is in the "Great Beyond" and Mama works nights to make ends meet for her brood of five in New

York City at the turn of the century. Christmas is approaching and Lili, 7, longs for a doll to replace her makeshift folded tea towel doll, but her hopes are not high. Mama sets them to work making paper ornaments for their donated Christmas tree, reminiscing all the while of her girlhood in Austria and of the events that have occurred to them as a family. On Christmas Eve while Mama is gone, a deliveryman brings a huge box that he admonishes them contains a lion. When Mama opens it on Christmas Day, the wonderful box disgorges treasures for them all, including dolls for Betty, 11, and Rosie, 9, clothing and toys for Ben, 5, and Sooch, 1, and at the very bottom a beautiful Chinese doll for Lili, all gifts from a chance acquaintance.

30. Doty, Jean Slaughter. <u>Gabriel</u>. New York: Macmillan, 1974. Illus. by Ted Lewin. Grades 4-6.

Linda finds life dull in the country where she and her mother, a freelance writer, have moved for economic reasons after her father's death. The discovery of an orphaned pup to nurture and the excitement of an afterschool job with a nearby kennel transform her life, but her happiness is ephemeral when the pup turns out to be a rare breed of show dog who belongs to someone else. Her disappointment in giving up Gabriel is ameliorated by her work at the kennels in helping groom and train him for showing. After he wins the coveted medal for Mrs. Wentworth, the owner, she shows her gratitude by transferring his registration papers to Linda's name.

31. Duncan, Lois. <u>Down a Dark Hall</u>. Boston: Little, Brown, 1974. Grades 6-8.

The night her father died seven years ago, Kit, now 14, saw him standing by her bed, but everyone insisted she had been dreaming. Now her mother has just remarried and while she and her new husband are honeymooning in Europe, Kit is parked at an exclusive boarding school run by a mysterious French woman and her son in a secluded, foreboding mansion. The four students have nothing in common but ESP and soon begin experiencing oppressive dreams and composing masterful poetry, paintings, music, and mathematical formulae far beyond their normal capacities. When they realize what is controlling their minds and the insidious consequences, they struggle to break the grasp but recognize that they are powerless prisoners of the evil headmistress. Pitting their wills against hers, they succeed in exorcising the spirits who, in a fit of pique, destroy Blackwood mansion, but Kit almost loses her life in saving that of another girl and is saved herself by her father's protective spirit.

32. Edmonds, Walter D. Two Logs Crossing. New York: Dodd, Mead, 1943. Illus. by Tibor Gergely. Grades 4-5.

John Haskell is 16 when his shiftless father dies, leaving six children, another on the way, and 40 dollars in debt to Judge Doane, an astronomical sum on the frontier in 1830. Determinedly, the boy hires himself out to farmers to support his family and reimburse the Judge, but it is agonizingly slow. Seth, a disreputable-looking Indian, offers to take him trapping for the winter, and he courageously asks the brusque Judge for a stake which is tersely granted. John learns a great deal from the Indian and accumulates a respectable pack of furs, but in his haste to market them and buy amenities for his mother he does not heed Seth's final admonition and loses his whole pack and very nearly his life when he tries to cross a roiling spring freshet on only one log. He faces the Judge manfully, and when the next trapping season approaches, the Judge volunteers to stake him again. His lesson learned the hard way, John makes good and redeems the Haskells' tarnished image.

33. Enright, Elizabeth. The Saturdays. New York: Holt, Rinehart and Winston, 1941. Illus. by the author. Grades 5-7.

The motherless Melendy menage is managed efficiently and benevolently by housekeeper Cuffy, handyman Willy, and Father, a busy professor of economics. Bored with dreary Saturdays in their aging and temperamental New York brownstone and cramped by meager allowances, the four resourceful and independent children decide to pool their assets so that each one can have a memorable experience of his choice every four weeks. Stagestruck Mona, 13, electrifies the family with a glamorous coiffure and manicure, musical Rush, 12, chooses an opera at Carnegie Hall, artistic Randy, 10, prefers an art exhibit, while 6-year-old Oliver naturally gravitates toward the circus. All get more than they bargained for. Among their adventures they acquire a dog and strike up a new rapport with an old friend, Mrs. Oliphant, who offers them an idyllic summer vacation in her very own lighthouse after an accidental fire in the attic makes a shambles of their stuffy city house.

34. _____. The Four-Story Mistake. New York: Holt, Rinehart and Winston, 1942. Illus. by the author. Grades 5-7.

Nostalgia for their comfortable old city house is swept away by delight in their new/old country home, an architect's nightmare but as unique as the four Melendy children, their father, Cuffy, Willy, and Isaac, the dog. Exploring the brook and woods by bicycle and ice skates, gifts from Mrs. Oliphant, provides hours of winter entertainment, but it is the cupola and concealed room with its unfolding mystery of the girl who once occupied it that really intrigues the children. A Christmas talent show leads to a radio acting job for Mona, and Rush teaches piano lessons to buy Defense Bonds. Randy makes her contribution by spying a real diamond in the brook, and Oliver discovers a treasure trove in the cellar.

35. _____. Then There were Five. New York: Holt, Rinehart and Winston, 1944. Illus. by the author. Grades 5-8.

It is summer vacation at the Four-Story Mistake [see 34] and Father is absent for long periods supporting the war effort in Washington. The precocious, imaginative, and versatile Melendy children dam the brook to create a swimming pool, conduct a scrap drive, befriend Mark, an orphan neighbor living with his malevolent second cousin, and with him share the adventures of swimming in an old quarry, searching for Indian arrowheads, and spelunking. When his cousin dies violently, the Melendys joyously and officially adopt Mark, and they cap the summer by staging a Children's Fair for charity.

36. _____. Spiderweb for Two: A Melendy Maze. New York: Holt, Rinehart and Winston, 1951. Grades 5-7.

The school year looms interminable to Oliver and Randy, the two youngest Melendys who are suffering from ennui as their older brothers and sister go away to school and Father returns to the lecture circuit. A trip to the mailbox produces a surprise message in the form of a rhyming riddle directing them to the next clue in a treasure hunt that they soon surmise will last all year. One verse points to another that seems to get progressively harder, leading them by trial and error, wit and hunch into intriguing and sometimes hazardous situations. They speculate on the author of the riddles but discover it only at the end of the rainbow trail, along with a special pot of gold from Mrs. Oliphant.

37. Estes, Eleanor. The Moffats. New York: Harcourt, Brace and World, 1941. Illus. by Louis Slobodkin. Grades 4-6.

 The yellow house on New Dollar Street in Cranbury lies under the shadow of a For Sale sign, but the inimitable Moffats, Sylvie, 15, Joe, 12, Jane, 9, Rufus, 5, and their seamstress mother make the best of it. Commonplace occurrences such as Rufus' first day of school, a saunter to Sunday school, and a junket to the beach assume an aura of adventure. Together they hatch a Halloween plot that thoroughly rattles the neighborhood bully. The boredom of quarantine (and another ominous sign on the house) when Rufus contracts scarlet fever is relieved by Mama's entrancing tales of her childhood in New York. The hovering spectre of privation during that grim winter fades into the background with the onset of spring, and the family moves into their tiny new house with the promise of a best friend for Jane.

38. _____. The Middle Moffat. New York: Harcourt, Brace and World, 1942. Illus. by Louis Slobodkin. Grades 4-6.

 The self-proclaimed "mysterious middle Moffat," shy, sensitive Jane, concocts her own cures for the middle-child syndrome. Blind faith and the luck o' the Irish help her muddle through them triumphantly. Her chief mission is to preserve the health of Cranbury's Oldest Inhabitant in anticipation of the spry and spirited fellow's hundredth birthday. An organ recital and a play at the Town Hall are rescued from the brink of disaster by spectacular quirks of fate, and when she ventures into basketball she simply cannot miss the basket! Together with her best friend Nancy, as gregarious and vivacious as Janey is bashful, she witnesses a solar eclipse and bathes stray dogs. The centenary birthday celebration inadvertently brings honor and glory to the modest Moffats through Jane.

39. _____. Rufus M. New York: Harcourt, Brace and World, 1943. Illus. by Louis Slobodkin. Grades 4-6.

The country is in the throes of World War, and the town of Cranbury, Connecticut, is contributing its share. The youngest Moffat, Rufus, 7, knits a somewhat grimy and ungainly washcloth for one of the boys in the trenches (and receives a treasured card of thanks clear from France), plants an eminently successful Victory Garden of green beans, and helps the rest of the intense and energetic Moffats make and market popcorn for Victory Buttons. But there's time for fun as well: his awed encounter with a player piano, a bittersweet Fourth of July, a spooky adventure at a deserted, fog-shrouded amusement park, an abortive attempt at ventriloquy, and a spectacular softball game of just one inning in which he saves his sister's team from disgrace. Rufus becomes the family hero on a bitter winter night when the water pipe bursts by propitiously producing the money to pay the plumber, buy more fuel, and provide supper all around.

40. Faber, Nancy W. Cathy at the Crossroads. Philadelphia: J. B. Lippincott, 1962. Illus. by Howard Simon. Grades 6-8.

Ten-year-old Cathy has been living complacently with her father and their faithful housekeeper since her mother's death and is naturally resentful when her father heavy-handedly springs a brand-new stepmother on her, expecting instant adoration. Barbara's every attempt at friendship is met with Cathy's resistance, in retaliation for her father's betrayal and in self-pity. The housekeeper is replaced by one of Barbara's choice, and a mysterious secret telephone line is installed in Barbara's study. Barbara redecorates Cathy's room in her favorite color and stages an elaborate and socially successful masquerade party for her birthday, winning Cathy's grudging approbation, and when the private telephone summons Barbara out on a frigid night, resulting in pneumonia, it evokes Cathy's incipient feelings of love for her stepmother. With the next enigmatic phone call, Cathy forces a confrontation and discovers Barbara's secret: the existence of her mentally retarded child. Cathy decides to accept the little girl as her sister and to live together as one felicitous family.

41. Farley, Carol. <u>The Garden Is Doing Fine</u>. New York: Atheneum, 1975. Illus. by Lynn Sweat. Grades 6-9.

Corrie's generous, impetuous, imaginative, and beloved father is dying of cancer at the close of World War II. He is like the frivolous flower in his cherished garden, while her sensible, pragmatic mother is more akin to the prosaic but vital vegetable. Corrie, 14, rails against a capricious fate that would pluck the bloom of such a kind and beautiful soul while sparing others less deserving and appreciative of life. She lights prayer candles at a Catholic church, reasoning that prayers that cost money are bound to be more efficacious than free Protestant ones. She experiences pangs of guilt when she recognizes her annoyance that his lingering illness is disturbing her social life. Her mother and an elderly neighbor help her to realize that when he is gone a part of him will be perpetuated in her and her brothers, and that as long as they remember him and speak of his memory, so long will he live. The physical garden may be dead and snow-shrouded, but the symbolic garden has been sown with strong seed, nurtured with love and integrity, and is free of the weeds of malice, pettiness, and discontent.

42. Fenton, Edward. <u>Duffy's Rocks</u>. New York: E. P. Dutton, 1974. Grades 5-8.

Gran Brennan reared the son on whom she doted, Timothy's father, so permissively that he grew up to be wild, restive, and irresponsible, stirred with the wanderlust that brought him to visit his motherless son, 13-year-old Tim, only once when he was 6. Gran is determined not to make the same mistake with Tim, who loves her in spite of her severity that precludes him from having friends outside of Duffy's Rocks, their dingy milltown suburb of Pittsburgh during the Great Depression. But Tim is longing to know this magnetic, enigmatic man who is his father. By stealth, he finds Bart Brennan's last known address, already two years old, among his grandmother's personal effects. Boarding a bus to New York, he traces Bart to a dead end, gaining insight into his character from two kind women he has discarded. Returning home he finds his grandmother on the brink of death, waiting to succumb only to extract Tim's promise not to follow in his father's footsteps, a pledge easily vowed.

43. Flory, Jane. The Golden Venture. Boston: Houghton Mifflin, 1976. Grades 5-6.

Eleven-year-old Minnie stows away on her father's wagon as he follows the Forty-niners to the California gold fields to make his fortune and establish his independence from his spinster sister so that he can remarry. He leaves Minnie in the care of a respectable woman with two daughters in the brawling shanty town of San Francisco. An independent young school teacher, sans school, joins their menage and turns entrepreneur, establishing a bakery in Mr. Haywood's Emporium and a laundry at the Stanhopes' house. The cash amasses, but a gang of felons, the Sydney Ducks, rapaciously pursue it. When Mr. Haywood is burned out, they all move to a berthed cargo ship abandoned by captain and crew, and there Minnie's father finds them, having lost his hoardings and his health. Minnie and Miss Daisy, the school marm, nurse him back to health, and together they put the Ducks to rout. Daisy and Mr. Welden decide to continue their reform campaign as husband and wife.

44. Fox, Paula. Portrait of Ivan. Englewood Cliffs, N.J.: Bradbury Press, 1969. Illus. by Saul Lambert. Grades 5-7.

Scores of photographs of 11-year-old Ivan adorn the home where he lives alone with his father, a busy executive who owns seven cameras, but curiously he has never seen a picture of his mother who died when he was a baby, and he is obsessed with the need to know more about his antecedents. All he knows of his mother is that she escaped her native Russia at the age of 3 in a horse-drawn sledge. When he goes to a painter's studio to sit for his portrait, he meets for the first time imaginative adults who take time to talk to a little boy and read aloud to him. His father gives him permission to go to Florida with the painter and his friend with the admonition to take plenty of pictures. There he meets a girl who introduces him to a wonderful outdoor world of boating, swimming, and jungle wildlife. He takes no photos, but his finished portrait captures his personality, as well as his appearance, better than any camera. Best of all is the painter's gift depicting his mother's escape party aboard the sledge--but peopled by his new friends and linking past with present.

Bibliography 69

45. _____. The Slave Dancer. Scarsdale, N.Y.: Bradbury Press, 1973. Illus. by Eros Keith. Grades 5-8.

On an errand for his mother, a New Orleans dressmaker, 13-year-old Jessie is hijacked along with his fife and carried aboard a slave ship bound for the coast of Africa. His duties are to kill rats, empty latrine buckets, and pipe music for the human cargo's exercise. Limber, muscular blacks commanded a better price in 1840 than flaccid ones. On the outbound voyage he is inducted into the brutality and inhumanity of the captain and crew, but nothing prepares him for the horrors of the homebound trip. About to consign the cargo to Spaniards in Cuba, the ship is caught by American authorities, and in the captain's frenzy to destroy the evidence, the slaves are all thrown to the sharks. Jessie and one boy cower in the noisome hold as a storm administers the wages of sin to ship and crew. Beached off the U.S. coast, Jessie finally makes his way home and the boy to safety in the North.

46. Freuchen, Pipaluk. Eskimo Boy. New York: Lothrop, Lee and Shepard, 1951. Illus. by Ingrid Vang Nyman. Grades 4-5.

Ivik watches in horror as his father is killed by a wounded walrus. As the family mourns, Ivik's kayak drifts away on the tide, leaving them stranded without means of livelihood on the barren island off the coast of Greenland where his father had taken them for the summer hunting season. The boy and his grandfather try to provide meat for the three younger children, but the old man is too feeble and the young one too inexperienced. They resort to eating their dog team, but soon the dogs are gone and they have only the harnesses to chew for sustenance. When the channel between the island and the mainland finally freezes, the starving Ivik sets out for help but is attacked by a savage polar bear which he manages to wound mortally. A company of fellow tribesmen comes upon him, and he returns home a hero with food, blubber and hides for his mother and family.

47. Garfield, Leon. Devil in the Fog. New York: Pantheon, 1966. Illus. by Antony Maitland. Grades 5-8.

A mystery story set in rural eighteenth-century England in which the eldest of the seven motherless Treets, a family of brilliant, ebullient, but improvident strolling entertainers, tumbles into apparent good fortune as the long-lost scion of a noble family. Adjustment to the life of gentility at their somber country seat is fraught first with frustrations for 14-year-old George and later with grave danger as he becomes embroiled in a sanguinary family feud, cloak and dagger intrigue, and finally mortal madness. He barely escapes with his life to rejoin his irrepressible true kindred who soon prosper with the aid of a surprising patroness.

48. Goudge, Elizabeth. Linnets and Valerians. New York: Coward-McCann, 1964. Illus. by Ian Ribbons. Grades 5-8.

In the year 1912, Father brings the four spirited, inquisitive Linnets, Nan, 12, Robert, 10, Timothy, 8, and Betsy, 6, home to England to live with his mother while he returns to his regiment in India via Egypt. Life with Grandmama and Miss Bolt seems intolerable, and the four lose no time in running away--straight into the arms of bombastic old Uncle Ambrose, a formidable curmudgeon, retired headmaster, and vicar of the village church. But the children sense that he's a benevolent tyrant and accept the challenge and adventure of living with him, adjusting to strict discipline and tough lessons. They also encounter danger and excitement with such colorful characters as reclusive Lady Alicia of mysterious Linden Manor and her monkey valet, gentle Daft Davie, wicked sorceress Emma Cobley, supernatural bees, and superstitious Ezra whose strong countermagic ends the skulduggery and enchantments and restores Lady Alicia's loved ones. Father also returns and all live happily, immortally, and Edwardianly ever after.

49. Gray, Elizabeth Janet. Jane Hope. New York: Viking Press, 1933. Grades 7-9.

Widowed Southern gentlewoman Mollie Lou Kennard takes her children, Mary Louise, 16, Jane Hope, 12, and Pierce, 9, to the convivial gentility of her ancestral home in the gracious antebellum college town of Chapel Hill, North Carolina, to live with her mother and father, a retired clergyman and benevolent slave owner. Mary Louise is a natural belle like her mother, but Jane Hope is an unabashed tomboy who seeks adventure and considers it a vexation to behave like the lady she is expected to be. She befriends a beleaguered freshman being hazed by sophomores, and she and Stephen become firm friends. Left at home as punishment for cropping her hair short, she rises to the occasion as hostess when handsome Cousin Flavellus comes to call, but when her mother wants to marry her girlhood beau, Jane Hope parries their happiness with her obstinate, selfish ambivalence. Later Stephen, now a junior of distinction, persuades her to reconsider. Suddenly he recognizes in his old chum a mature poise and beauty at 15 and asks her to wear his fraternity pin as he goes whirling off to the Civil War.

50. Gray, Patsey. Star Bright. New York: W. W. Norton, 1964. Grades 6-8.

Deb is Starstruck over her wonderful colt, given to her by a neighboring horse-breeder because he lacks a pedigree. Deb's mother, however, sees only the costly destructive potential of the spoiled and undisciplined young stallion (her husband died of horse-inflicted injuries at their modest boarding stable in the Santa Cruz Mountains of California). Star must be sold, but prospective buyers, aware of his reputation as a rogue, are leery. Deb solves the problem by giving Star back to the original owners for their grandson to ride. When this arrangement fails, Star Bright must be transported to the state fair for sale on a "one-way ticket." Unexpected occurrences at the fair save Star from the auction block and bring good fortune to the Bell family in the form of stud fees.

51. _____. Star Lost. New York: W. W. Norton, 1965. Grades 6-8.

Deb and her best friend Maureen gain permission to camp by themselves for an entire week in the Santa Cruz Mountains with their horses, Star Bright and the balky pony Patches. Star's canine bosom buddy, Blackie, follows them and has to be returned and locked up. That night Star, carelessly tethered and obeying his instincts, slips his hobble and runs off, with Patches close behind, seeking Blackie. When the girls awake in the morning and discover their loss they set off in remorseful pursuit. The two horses lead them a merry chase which leads to grave danger when they staunchly lend protection to a heifer and her helpless calf stalked by a coyote pack, compensating for their earlier negligence. Deb learns that love and loyalty can be shared; they don't have to be divided.

The Single-Parent Family

52. Greenfield, Eloise. <u>Sister</u>. New York: Thomas Y. Crowell, 1974. Illus. by Moneta Barrett. Grades 5-7.
    Folks notice the physical resemblance between Doretha, 13, and her scapegrace sister, Alberta, 16, but fail to note the difference in personalities. Doretha is as proud and positive as Alberta is narrow and negative. Returning home to her black ghetto in Washington, D. C., from a rock concert, Doretha records her sensations in her diary, then reviews the earlier major entries back to the year she was 9 and received the diary from her father. Recorded are her father's death, the story of her great-great-grandfather, who was a slave, the gift of the flute and another lesson in bereavement, the substitute teacher who almost sowed the seeds of hatred, the day of her resilient mother's second heartbreak, the afterschool African school instilling pride, the first time her sister ran away. Here is the fabric of her life, the fiber of her heritage that shaped her strength and individuality but sapped her sister's because she failed to perceive it.

53. Harnett, Cynthia. <u>The Great House</u>. Cleveland: World Publishing, 1949. Illus. by the author. Grades 6-8.
    In the summer of 1690, their architect father, commissioned to design a grand manor for a country gentleman, takes Geoffrey and Barbara with him to Ladybourne, away from noisy, malodorous London. Father is obliged to return on business almost immediately but allows them to stay with the nearby innkeeper. They make friends with the daughter of the estate and her grandmother but are frightened of her mad French nursemaid. Geoffrey, whose ambition is to become an architect and attend Oxford, takes his father's plans and lays them out on a more advantageous site than that of the old hall and later saves the old hall from destruction by fire. The grateful squire, returning from abroad, underwrites Geoffrey's desire for education and arranges for Barbara to live with his family as companion to his daughter. The life and accoutrements of the times are depicted in copious illustrations.

54. Hegan, Alice Caldwell. <u>Mrs. Wiggs of the Cabbage Patch</u>. New York: Century, 1901. Grades 4-6.
    Indefatigable Mrs. Wiggs remains cheerful and hopeful despite every cruel trick fate deals her: loss of husband "by the alcohol route," death by starvation of her elder son and provider, pestilence and deprivation.

Divine Providence in the guise of a beautiful benefactress and a handsome hedonist intervenes to save her and the younger children, Asia, Australia, Europena--and Billy, proving once again that virtue, patience, and faith are amply rewarded. Hedonist, of course, succumbs to blandishments of benefactress, forswears his former ways, and wins his suit.

55. Heide, Florence Parry. <u>Growing Anyway Up</u>. Philadelphia: J. B. Lippincott, 1976. Grades 6-9.

Florence's father died when she was too young to remember him well, but she has remained intense, introverted, and pathologically insecure inside the protective shell she has so deliberately and painstakingly erected between herself and the threatening outside world. Her mother's decision to move from their secure routine in Florida near the soothing sea to a new apartment in Pennsylvania, a new school, new classmates, and a pompous new boyfriend for her mother aggravates her condition because she cannot tolerate the dangers of change. The spells and incantations she employs to ward them off give her the appearance of having nervous tics, and she is suspected of being psychotic. Only her extrovert aunt understands her and begins to draw her out, but her aunt's sudden departure threatens to topple her teetering emotional balance while it triggers a memory of repressed guilt over her father's death--which once articulated becomes the bottom rung on the ladder to maturity.

56. Hunt, Irene. <u>Up a Road Slowly</u>. Chicago: Follett, 1966. Illus. by Don Bolognese. Grades 5-8.

Julie is 7 when her mother dies and she and her 9-year-old brother are wrenched from their home in town to live in the country with their reserved, cultivated spinster aunt and suave, sarcastic, alcoholic uncle, leaving 17-year-old Laura to keep house for Father, a college professor. Aunt Cordelia is also their school teacher, and Julie is frequently bitterly resentful of her inflexibility and devotion to duty and longs for a future when she can return to the security of her own home and family. But when her brother is sent to boarding school, her sister marries and has children of her own, and Father remarries, she realizes that Father's house is no longer the home she remembers. Over the years she has become quite fond of her undemonstrative aunt and chooses to remain with her, commuting to high school in town. An unfortunate infatuation with a boy who wants to exploit her almost spoils her relationship with her childhood beau, but Uncle Haskell intervenes before it goes too far, one of his few constructive acts. Julie and Danny finally declare their mutual affection, and Julie, class valedictorian, prepares to go off to the state university.

57. Hunter, Mollie. A Sound of Chariots. New York: Harper and Row, 1972. Grades 6-9.

Disabled in World War I, Bridie's father espouses the cause of socialism, stumping for reform for invalided veterans and tenant farmers in neo-feudalistic post-war Scotland. Bridie, next to the youngest of the family's five children, idolizes her father, grows up in his image, and is the apple of his eye. She is 9 at the time of his death, and her torment knows no bounds. She despises her fundamentalist mother's lachrymose grief and desolation but can find no acceptable channel for her own which surfaces in terrifying nightmares. In trying to explain the finality of death to her little brother she perceives her own mortality and decides she cannot waste a moment of the time remaining to her, but in trying to find her niche she only succeeds in understanding and appreciating her mother more. Her poetry is encouraged for its expressiveness but discountenanced because it is unprofitable until one perceptive professor tells her, "You are your father's daughter--live for him!" The exigency of making a living is paramount, but she can devote her spare time to liberating the poetry in her mind.

58. Johnson, Annabel, and Edgar Johnson. The Black Symbol. New York: Harper and Row, 1959. Grades 5-8.

When 12-year-old Barney runs away from his unkind cousins in search of his prospector father in Gold Rush days, it seems providential that he should fall in with Dr. Cathcart's traveling Miracle Show, but gradually the truth begins to dawn on the gullible boy that Dr. Cathcart is not only a charlatan and a cheat but a nefarious despot who resorts to chicanery to enslave him forever as a helpless shill. Befriended by the show's blind, sullen strongman, a slave in body but not in mind, the pair attempts an escape that leads to the capture of the blind giant with the prospect of physical and spiritual torture as punishment. Resourcefully surviving in the wilderness, Barney eventually finds his father and the

Bibliography

two plot to unmask the mountebank while freeing Steve and Billy, the subjugated black juggler. The liberated trio and their emancipator become partners in a copper-mining venture when silver peters out and are destined to make their fortunes. Barney learns not to accept appearances or the printed word at face value.

59. _____, and _____. A Golden Touch. New York: Harper and Row, 1963. Grades 6-8.

    Andy was reared by his maternal grandparents after his mother's death at his birth, but now that his grandmother is dead and his grandfather is entering the Civil War Veterans' Home, Andy, 13, must go to live with his footloose father or be sent to an orphanage. His initial encounter with his inscrutable father and indolent uncle is unsettling when he learns that they are both dodging the law and existing by their wits in the toughest gold mining town west of Denver. Their fortunes soon improve when they become partners in a mining venture with a wily old prospector who supplies the capital, a finicky Frenchman who furnishes the mine, and an ex-dancehall girl who mothers them all. But the sheriff doggedly harasses them, and Andy has the uneasy feeling that his father is a crook. In the harrowing denouement, deep within the mine, it unfolds that Andy's uncle is the real malefactor and that his father had been protecting his avaricious brother until he overstepped the bounds of kinship and decency by defrauding the partnership and planning Andy's demise. In mutual trust, father and son ride off into the sunset.

60. Lampman, Evelyn Sibley. The Shy Stegosaurus of Cricket Creek. Garden City, N.Y.: Doubleday, 1955. Illus. by Paul Galdone. Grades 4-6.

    Willed a ranch by a great-uncle, the fatherless Brown family give up city life with high hopes of becoming prosperous ranchers, but the desolate, arid terrain will grow nothing but sagebrush. An absent-minded professor of archaeology offers them a temporary reprieve by boarding with them for the summer while hunting for dinosaur fossils. Young Joan and Joey have no luck finding fossils but colossal luck in locating a real live Stegosaurus named George, who has survived by adapting his diet to sagebrush. George is shy and not too bright, but he is loyal and helpful. With his aid the children clear the land of sagebrush, catch a bank robber, earn the reward, locate valuable fossils, not of dinosaurs but of a prehistoric horse, save the ranch, and incidentally stumble into hilarious hot water.

61. Lewis, Elizabeth Foreman. <u>Young Fu of the Upper Yangtze</u>. New York: Holt, Rinehart and Winston, 1932. Illus. by Kurt Wiese. Grades 5-7.

  Young Fu, 14, and his mother, a farmer's widow, come to Chungking where he is apprenticed to Tang Coppersmith. The country boy endures the mockery of fellow apprentices, makes bonds of friendship with Small Li, earns the jealousy and animosity of Den and the respect of his employer. Sent on errands about the city, he observes the barbarity of soldiers, the wretchedness of professional beggars, and the ruthlessness of organized bandits. Twice in his naivete he is bilked by crafty flatterers, in a pawn shop and in a gambling den. He saves the missionaries' hospital from fire and lays to rest his superstitious fear of foreign devils and dragons of ill fortune. He foils a burglary attempt by a former disgruntled employee and proves the innocence of another employee falsely accused of drug trafficking. When his enemy Den casts suspicion of theft on Fu, Tang places his trust in Fu, now 19 and a journeyman, and adopts him as his son. His mother will never want again.

62. Madison, Winifred. <u>Marinka, Katinka and Me (Susie)</u>. Scarsdale, N.Y.: Bradbury Press, 1975. Illus. by Miller Pope. Grades 3-5.

  The three new girls in class gravitate toward one another on their first day of fourth grade and soon become inseparable companions, jumping rope, playing dress-up, talking on the telephone, going to a birthday party, walking their identical puppies, wearing their identical knit caps, and dancing a special Maidens' Dance at a school performance. Blonde Marinka's mother is divorced, brunette Susie's father is dead, while red-tressed Katinka's father is in prison. One day a silly quarrel pairs Susie and Marinka against Katinka who now walks home from school on the opposite side of the street. Then Susie and Katinka patch their misunderstanding and it is Marinka's turn to be odd-man-out. The Ouija board suggests to Susie and Katinka that Marinka is sad and lonely, and the two agree that it takes three to jump rope successfully. The olive branch is extended and the argument forgotten.

Bibliography

63. Mathis, Sharon Bell. <u>Listen for the Fig Tree.</u> New York: Viking Press, 1974. Grades 7-9.

    The dark world of 16-year-old Muffin, blind of glaucoma since 10, consists of her mother who finds forgetfulness in a bottle since her husband's violent death last Christmas Eve, her boyfriend Ernie, a devout Black Muslim, and Mr. Dale, their upstairs neighbor who loves her like a father and treats her royally. Her major concerns are, first, to guide her mother safely past the anniversary of her father's death, a seemingly hopeless battle in which their roles are reversed and Muffin loses some odious skirmishes, and second, to celebrate her first black African Kwanza on Christmas night, a more attainable goal even though she doesn't have a suitable dress to wear. Ernie insists that it is how you feel, not what you wear that is important, but Mr. Dale provides the material and she sews her own stunning costume. The traumatic attempted rape in which the dress is ruined almost causes her to miss the Kwanza, but with Ernie's and Mr. Dale's support she overcomes her fears and experiences the beauty and unity of the ancient black pageant which inspires strength to struggle on with her mother.

64. Meigs, Cornelia. <u>Wind in the Chimney.</u> New York: Macmillan, 1934. Illus. by Louise Mansfield. Grades 4-6.

    The fatherless Moreland family, recent emigrants from England, take up residence in the unoccupied Bayard farmhouse in the Pennsylvania countryside in the early days of the Republic. Enterprising Richard, 14, soon finds a berth with a wagoner freighting goods to Pittsburgh, gateway to the West. But it is Mother's fine weaving that gains Debby, 8, entree to Philadelphia society and the magnate who owns the property where they live with the glimmer of hope that in his generosity he will let them stay on. But Mr. Bayard's sister wants Cherry Hill farm as a wedding gift for her daughter. Only the presentation of a rare wheel of fortune-patterned coverlid would please her more. Contacted by messenger, Richard finds a 100-year-old pattern, and Mrs. Moreland and Debby work at the loom around the clock to finish the intricate quilt in time for the wedding. Cherry Hill farm becomes theirs, and Debby and President and Mrs. Washington are fellow wedding guests.

65. Moon, Grace. Chi-Wee. Garden City, N. Y.: Doubleday, 1925. Illus. by Carl Moon. Grades 5-6.

Chi-Wee, the plump 7-year-old Pueblo Indian girl who lives alone with her poor mother on the mesa, accidentally discovers rare pottery clay for her mother's jars, is saved from kidnapping by her pet goat, brings a thief to earth, earns a beautiful shawl for her mother, is rescued from drowning in a flash flood by a Navaho boy, is rewarded for her part in flushing a bear, is chastised for defiling the Kiva out of curiosity, makes a trip with her aunt to the cliff dwellings to make her first jar and receive a symbolic ring, accepts precious turquoises for saving the life of an old man, finds a stolen baby on the desert and is loath to part with it, but when the rightful father is located she discovers to her joy that he and her mother have married and she has a new father and baby brother!

66. Nash, Mary. While Mrs. Coverlet was Away. Boston: Little, Brown, 1958. Illus. by Garrett Price. Grades 4-6.

When their energetic, vitamin-peddling father flies off to New Zealand to supervise an inherited derelict tin mine, and their housekeeper hies off to Duluth to manage her daughter's household when she breaks a leg, the three Persever children, Malcolm, Molly, and Theobald, whose sobriquet is Toad, resort to subterfuge to camouflage Mrs. Coverlet's absence so the three can remain together and independent for the summer. Their most pressing problem is for a means of livelihood when the money their father left in the bank runs out. The Toad saves the day when his cat turns out to be a rare male tortoise shell which a New York cat fancier pays a princely price for. The 6-year-old Toad then concocts a sauce with a secret ingredient to tempt his new cat that becomes popular all over town and further fills their coffers. The game is up when the secret ingredient is exhausted and the neighbors become suspicious, but they are saved from separation by the return of their father and Mrs. Coverlet, and all is forgiven.

67. Ness, Evaline. Sam, Bangs and Moonshine. New York: Holt, Rinehart and Winston, 1966. Illus. by the author. Grades 2-3.

Samantha invents stories to compensate for the loss of her mother but can't sort fact from fancy. She tells her very literal friend Thomas that her mother is a mermaid and that she has a lion and a baby kangaroo for pets instead of an ordinary cat named Bangs. When she sends Thomas on a wild goose chase to Blue Rock to look for the kangaroo, she comes to the sudden realization that the tide will soon cover the rock and sweep Thomas with it. Her fisherman father rescues him but cannot save Bangs who was with Thomas. The remorseful Sam sobs herself to sleep, but bedraggled Bangs belatedly appears, and she ruefully resolves to separate reality from fantasy without submerging the vivid imagination her father calls "moonshine." In the morning he presents her with a gerbil that looks like a baby kangaroo which she in turn bestows on Thomas. She names it Moonshine.

68. Ormondroyd, Edward. <u>Time at the Top</u>. Berkeley, Calif.: Parnassus Press, 1963. Illus. by Peggie Bach. Grades 5-6.

On one of those days when everything goes wrong, Susan stops to assist a frazzled old woman and for her trouble is told she may have three, but the crone neglects to say three what. Later, in the apartment building where she resides with her father, the erratic old elevator fails to stop at the top floor but continues through time to deposit her in a Victorian drawing room in the year 1881. There she makes friends with Vicky and Robert, children of the wealthy widow who lives there, and together they conspire to prevent Mrs. Walker from marrying Mr. Sweeney, a bounder and fortune-hunter. Susan's performance convinces Mr. Sweeney that Mrs. Walker has lost her inheritance and has contracted smallpox as well. The first part is prophetic because the assets are indeed gone. A twentieth-century newspaper clipping, however, directs the children to buried treasure, replacing the fickle fiduciary funding. Susan is enamored of the past and schemes to get her father on the elevator. He agrees [see 69] only if she will promise to see a psychiatrist afterward.

69. _____. <u>All in Good Time</u>. Berkeley, Calif.: Parnassus Press, 1975. Illus. by Ruth Robbins. Grades 6-8.

To humor Susan who he believes has had a mental aberration, Mr. Shaw agrees to accompany her on the elevator to 1881 [see 68]. The anticipated instant romance does not bud on his first meeting with Mrs.

Walker, and he is determined to return to the twentieth century, thus squandering the final magical elevator time trip and plunging the children into despair. The appearance of Cousin Jane, a termagant who tyrannizes all the Walkers, delays their return, and the reappearance of villainous Mr. Sweeney, a professional bluebeard, convinces Mr. Shaw, suddenly smitten by the hapless widow's charms, to stay. He and the children connive to bring the scoundrel to justice, but their plot goes awry. A random rendezvous in the candlelit corridor bestows a monumental surprise on Mr. Sweeney and Cousin Jane: a long, one-way ride to the future in an unconventional conveyance.

70. Polland, Madeleine. <u>The White Twilight</u>. New York: Holt, Rinehart and Winston, 1962. Illus. by Alan Cober. Grades 6-8.

Reared in sixteenth-century austerity by her Flemish aunt, at 12 Hanne is sent to live at the Danish court at Elsinore where her father has been commissioned to design the magnificent Kronborg castle. She struggles to be a dutiful daughter to the father she has placed on a pedestal, and resists the efforts of Carl Adam, the nettlesome but magnetic nobleman's son, who tries occasionally to tease her from her own pedestal of rigid conditioning and hauteur. One night he persuades her to sail across the straits to Sweden on a dangerous secret mission, embroiling her in the political plot in which he is a double agent with loyalty divided between his true father, a Robin Hood of pirates, and his uncle, as whose son he poses, a favorite of the Crown. It is she who persuades him to look at his father objectively in the long twilight of the northern summer. When the time comes he renounces the world and joins the ascetic life of the famous astronomer Tycho Brahe, while she resolves to relax her stiff standards and wins paternal approbation.

71. Sawyer, Ruth. <u>The Year of Jubilo</u>. New York: Viking Press, 1940. Illus. by Edward Shenton. Grades 7-8.

Tomboy Lucinda, now 14, of the author's Newbery Award-winning <u>Roller Skates</u>, returns under far different circumstances. Her father has just died and the family has lost its assets in the Depression. She, her three elder brothers, and their fragile mother are forced to abandon New York and live the year around in their summer cottage on the coast of Maine under severely straitened conditions. Carter, 18, makes it difficult for

Lucinda with his pejorative pokes, but she pitches in by learning to cook. Each of the brothers contributes to their livelihood, but the Stygian winter weather is more than they bargained for and Mother takes pneumonia and nearly dies. But they all prove their mettle and manage a little merriment along the way with good neighbors. Lucinda befriends the ambitious daughter of a shiftless family, participates in the capture of a gang of thieves, falls in love and gets an awful jolt, engineers a surprise wedding for Duncan, and eventually makes peace with Carter.

72. Shannon, Monica. <u>Dobry</u>. New York: Viking Press, 1934. Illus. by Atanas Katchamakoff. Grades 6-9.

 Young Dobry dreams of being a great artist and spends all his spare time drawing pictures. His grandfather encourages his ambition, declaring that it has been prophesied that he will grow up to have the fire of God in him, but his pragmatic mother thinks he should take his dead peasant father's place in the fields. She changes her mind when the boy sculpts an inspirational nativity scene in the snow by the stable, and he is given the job of herding cows to free him from field work so he can practice his art. Over the years as he hones his talent, the three of them partake with gusto of the seasonal events of their Bulgarian village: the annual journey to the milltown at harvest, the coming of the Gypsy Bear, Grandfather's victory in the Snow-Melting Game and his prowess at story-telling. To earn money for his formal training, Dobry proves his physical endurance by diving in icy water for the golden crucifix in the traditional February ceremony before his departure for Sofia, but he promises his childhood sweetheart that he will return to her.

73. Sidney, Margaret. <u>Five Little Peppers</u>. New York: Macmillan, 1962 (c1880). Illus. by Anna Marie Magagna. Grades 6-8.

 Good fortune, like manna from Heaven, showers the impoverished but high-principled Peppers and their Mamsie after the whole family nearly dies of measles and baby Phronsie, 4, is kidnapped by an organ grinder. Kindly Dr. Fisher provides a new stove for the "Little Brown House," and Jasper, Phronsie's rescuing swain, and his irascible but benevolent father supply the Peppers with their first real Christmas, an opportunity for education, and finally a sumptuous abode and long-lost cousins, all served up in cloying, hyperbolic Victorian sentiment.

74. Snyder, Zilpha Keatley. <u>The Egypt Game.</u> New York: Atheneum, 1968. Illus. by Alton Raible. Grades 5-6.

Eleven-year-old April's ambitious show business mother sends her to live with her paternal grandmother, her father having been killed in Korea, while she awaits her big break. In spite of her false eyelashes and Hollywood affectations, she makes friends with Melanie, a girl her age who lives downstairs, because she is imaginative and likes to read. Finding a plaster bust of Nefertiti in the cluttered yard of an antique dealer, they conceive their Egypt Game, recruiting Melanie's little brother Marshall as boy pharaoh Marshamosis and a new girl, Elizabeth, as Neferbeth. When a child in the neighborhood is foully murdered, everyone suspects the gruff old man who is proprietor of the shop in whose yard they play. Two boys, erstwhile bullies, join the Egyptians at Halloween, and the Game gets spookier as the Oracle of Thoth begins speaking mysteriously. April almost becomes the murderer's victim, and the Egypt Game terminates suddenly. When April's mother marries her agent, April finally realizes that she never intended to send for her and accepts with dignity her new life.

75. Sperry, Armstrong. <u>Call it Courage.</u> New York: Macmillan, 1940. Illus. by the author. Grades 4-6.

Mafatu was christened Stout Heart by his father, a noble Polynesian chief before the days of traders and missionaries, but after the sea claimed his mother and almost snuffed his life when he was 3, the villagers began to call him the Boy Who Was Afraid because he feared the sea. When all the other boys embark on the annual bonito run only Mafatu, 15, stays behind to craft tools, woman's work. His cowardice shames him, and with sudden resolve he determines to prove himself or die trying. With his dog Uri for company, he puts to sea in an outrigger where he is at the mercy of the enemy sea god Moana and the friendly god of fishermen, Maui. A titanic storm robs him of sail, tools, food and clothing, and he nearly dies of exposure before his pet albatross directs him to land. There he proves his courage and ingenuity by designing new tools and canoe, killing a shark, octopus and wild boar in mortal combat, but most of all by daring to steal the sacred spear from the shrine of the eaters-of-men and living to tell the tale. He returns to his village victorious, worthy of the title Stout Heart, and a credit to his father.

76. Spykman, E. C. <u>A Lemon and a Star</u>. New York: Harcourt, Brace and World, 1955. Grades 5-8.

On her tenth birthday in 1907, Jane Cares receives an ignominious lemon from her mischievous brother Ted, 13, and witnesses an auspicious falling star, auguring an eventful summer of adventure and misadventure for the four irrepressible children, including Edie, 5, and Hubert, 8. Left largely to their own devices with a retinue of servants in attendance, they are not prissy products of privilege but free spirits who use their intrepid imaginations and boundless energy to rescue a trapped fox, foil a thief by main strength and cunning, fall in the reservoir maelstrom from the creaky catwalk, nearly get killed by hornet stings, save their father from death at the hands of a villain bent on revenge, make an unauthorized trip to the city to see the sights, engineer a hazardous steeplechase, and collect mud, blood and bruises in intracameral strife. When Father brings home a new wife, the younger children are won over immediately, but Ted displays stubborn defiance until "Madam" saves him from severe punishment at his father's hand.

77. Steele, William O. <u>Winter Danger</u>. New York: Harcourt, Brace and World, 1954. Illus. by Paul Galdone. Grades 4-6.

Since his Ma's death, footloose Pa takes 11-year-old Caje along on his peregrinations as a "woodsy," hunting and trapping to eke a living from the wilderness. Pa thinks he is a chip off the block, but Caje secretly yearns for the comfort of a dry cabin with a warm fire and soft bed. A hair-raising encounter with hostile Indians only exhilarates Pa, but a mass aerial migration of squirrels portending a severe winter sobers him into seeking shelter with his brother-in-law's family, relatives Caje has never met. Pa becomes restless in the settlers' cabin and soon strikes out on his own, leaving Caje an object of charity, unfamiliar with farm chores and irked by a contentious cousin. The winter lives up to expectations, and when his uncle sickens and they face starvation, Caje braves the Arctic chill to kill a bear and stave off a pack of wolves for its life-sustaining meat, casting his lot with his adoptive family.

84   The Single-Parent Family

78. _____. The Year of the Bloody Sevens. New York: Harcourt, Brace and World, 1963. Illus. by Charles Beck. Grades 4-6.

   In the year 1777, 11-year-old Kelsey, who has been living with neighbors since his mother's death, receives a letter from his father telling him to join him in Kentucky, the wild frontier. At first he travels with a family group, but they make little headway because of the cattle they are herding, so he joins forces with a pair of obstreperous "woodsies" with whom he can scarcely keep up. The woodsies are ambushed and annihilated by Indians, and Kel has to run for his life, but though he escapes he is utterly lost in the wilderness with a rifle but no powder horn. He presses ever westward, looking for outposts of civilization, dodging fearsome Indians, bears and snakes, and almost succumbing to starvation before he descries the stockade where his father is waiting for him. Pa helps him assuage his feeling of guilt over the deaths of the woodsies.

79. Stephens, Mary Jo. Witch of the Cumberlands. Boston: Houghton Mifflin, 1974. Illus. by Arvis Stewart. Grades 6-9.

   Dr. McGregor brings his teenage daughters, cautious Susan, 17, and impulsive Betsy, 15, and inscrutable son Robin, 4, to the peace and beauty of the Cumberland Mountains of Kentucky because the pressure of life in New York has been too great since his wife's death. He immediately embroils them in a forty-year-old mystery in which they are the catalysts to a suspenseful denouement along with Miss Birdie, the elderly herbalist and fortune teller; Broughton, the foreboding figure in black; and the spirit of the dead coal miner who rises from his dank grave to exact his retribution and bare the culpability for the mine disaster that killed 49 men during the Depression. In the meantime they learn to accept and be accepted by "holler" folk and townfolk alike, understand the alliance of magic, superstition, simple faith, and inspired evangelical oratory that comprise religion in the hills, deplore the exploitation of the mountain region and people, and develop an appreciation for the uncanny gifts of Miss Birdie and clairvoyant Robin.

80. Stolz, Mary. The Edge of Next Year. New York: Harper and Row, 1974. Grades 6-9.

   The shattering tragedy of their mother's death in an auto accident affects 14-year-old Orin, his 10-year-old brother Victor, and their journalist father differently. Orin is puzzled and resentful of Victor's seeming indifference to the mutual loss in his absorption with his hobbies, and appalled and disgusted with his father's increasing immersion in alcoholism. Sensitive and introspective, he misses his unique mother despairingly and evokes her memory constantly, while at the same time shouldering the overwhelming responsibility for brother, father, home, and personal life. After the disposal of his mother's effects, he makes a determined effort to come to grips with his sorrow, recalling that in response to his query, "in the end you'd have to say that what a person feels doesn't matter at all, " his mother replied, "It matters; it's just not all that matters. " In the end he summons the courage to shock his father into seeking help for his drinking problem.

81. Talbot, Toby. Away Is So Far. New York: Four Winds Press, 1974. Illus. by Dominique Michelle Strandquest. Grades 4-5.

Despite 11-year-old Pedro's pleas that problems can't be solved by running away from them, his distraught father is driven by grief to leave his farm and village on the Mediterranean coast of Spain after his wife's death and become a wandering minstrel or tocador. Pedro remembers his mother's adjuration to live normally after her death, but it does not deter his adamant father, and after stopping to buy him sturdy shoes, they strike the open road, sleeping under the stars at night and playing the guitar for meals. They ply their way by train to Paris where it is rumored that Spanish guitarists are in demand. There his father finds not the forgetfulness he seeks but a return to reason, and he is able to face with equanimity once again the cheerful little house with its myriad memories.

82. Taylor, Theodore. Teetoncey. Garden City, N. Y.: Doubleday, 1974. Illus. by Richard Cuffari. Grades 5-6.

The independent, insular folk indigenous to North Carolina's Outer Banks have witnessed the foundering of countless vessels on their treacherous shoals, but being the descendants of castaways themselves they have not been inured to human suffering. When 11-year-old Ben finds a half-drowned girl, sole survivor of another shipwreck, on the beach one stormy night in 1898, his mother, who lost a husband and son to the sea, insists on taking her in and caring for her. The girl recovers physically but her mind remains in a catatonic trance, blocking out all memory of the tragedy in which her parents perished. Nicknamed Teetoncey, meaning small in the peculiar Banks patois, she is mutely and unemotionally docile and allows Ben, her reluctant escort, to lead her about. But when she wanders off alone and becomes a danger to herself, Ben's mother devolves on him a desperate scheme of restoring her to reason. On a violently stormy night, he leads her back to the beach. The re-creation by demonic wind and wave of the initial trauma breaks the barrier, and her emotions flood forth in normal reaction.

83. _____. Teetoncey and Ben O'Neal. Garden City, N. Y.: Doubleday, 1975. Illus. by Richard Cuffari. Grades 5-7.

When the castaway Teetoncey girl is catapulted from her catatonia [see 82] and reveals that she has no living relatives, Ben's mother is determined to keep her for the daughter she always wanted, out of the clutches of the cantankerous consul who wants to return her to her native London, and Ben sees the opportunity to cut the apron strings and go to sea as his brothers and father before him. He changes his mind when Teetoncey discloses to him privately that she is an heiress and that her fortune lies under the shallow waters and shifting sands of the shoals where she was shipwrecked. The youths' efforts to recover the legacy goes awry and doesn't remain a secret for long. Soon a full-scale salvage operation is mounted, the spoils hotly contested. Ben's mother sees to it that if it cannot be restored to the rightful owner, no one shall profit by it, but the effort costs her life. Ben and Tee have grown fond of one another, but sadly know they must part: Teetoncey to return to England; Ben to fulfill his destiny at sea.

84. Ullman, James Ramsey. Banner in the Sky. Philadelphia: J. B. Lippincott, 1954. Grades 6-9.

Sixteen-year-old Rudi's father, the greatest mountaineer in Switzerland, died in attempting to scale the Citadel, the last unconquered Alp, which the author has modeled on the Matterhorn. It is Rudi's dream to finish his father's business, but his mother and uncle have forbidden him to climb. By concealing his rude equipment he manages to practice clandestinely, and when he saves the life of a great British alpinist, the astute veteran recognizes the boy's spirit and potential. Rudi's fearful mother remains immutably opposed to his ambition, and he resorts to subterfuge to join the Englishman's expedition. Against all odds, the lad finds the elusive route past the obdurate obstacle that even his father failed to discern fifteen years before, and leads the party against the panoply of dangers and endurance tests a chimerical mountain can hurl at mere mortals. He is bitterly thwarted yards short of the summit in coming to the aid of an injured adversary, but the adulatory Englishman plants Rudi's father's pennon atop the peak and predicts that he will climb it often, while his mother ruefully removes her oppostion.

85. Voight, Virginia F. Apple Tree Cottage. New York: Holiday House, 1949. Illus. by Eloise Wilkin. Grades 4-6.

    Motherless Susan, 14, and Candy, 9, set up housekeeping in an abandoned house in the Pennsylvania countryside in the year 1842 when their father, an itinerant painter, falls ill. Over an idyllic summer they find and befriend a lost boy, solve a crime, restore their father to health, and color mezzotints for Mr. Godey's magazine. The grateful owner of the retrieved stolen property recognizes Father's talents and puts him under commission, and with the malefactor behind bars, their orphaned friend comes out of hiding and gives them possession of the house.

86. Walter, Mildred Pitts. Lillie of Watts. Los Angeles: Ward Ritchie Press, 1969. Illus. by Leonora E. Prince. Grades 3-5.

    Lillie, next-to-youngest of the family of eight, who has to share a room with her mother and 5-year-old brother, wears her good sweater to school on the day of her eleventh birthday against her mother's better judgment and accidentally ruins it in art class. Her mother cancels the treat of taking her to the beach home of the lady she cleans for. That evening she brings home the lady's exotic cat to keep overnight, but Lillie is afraid the cat is evil and will kill her because of a superstition her grandmother told her. In the middle of the night she lets it out of the house, and then Mama is really angry, telling her not to come back till she finds it. When she returns unsuccessful, Mama relents and tells her that people are more important than animals. Brother Eddie finds the cat, Lillie's fears are ameliorated, and she becomes a cat lover.

87. Wayne, Kyra Petrovskaya. The Witches of Barguzin.
Nashville: Thomas Nelson, 1975. Grades 7-9.
This is the poignant and chilling saga of the romance between Lubasha and Vasily whose violently widowed mothers are cast by cruel fate upon the edge of the vast, desolate Siberian taiga. Lubasha's mother, mute and demented from witnessing her husband's murder and the torching of their home by an ignorant, barbarous peasantry, finds refuge with an elderly ascetic at his hermitage in the trackless forest, domain of marauding wolves and bears. Vasily's mother, a cultured and sensitive political exile, was banished to the hostile, illiterate village for anti-Czarist activities after the hanging of her husband. Their ostracized children naturally gravitate toward one another. Eventually this mutual affection deepens into a love affair, but the association endangers all their lives. Vasily is beaten senseless when he warns Lubasha and her mother, now reduced to an infantile state by her insanity, that the brutal, superstitious villagers are coming to kill them, but when his mother receives her reprieve and returns to civilization, he chooses to remain behind with Lubasha to live the life of primitive seclusion and subsistence inculcated by the old recluse.

88. Webb, Christopher. Quest of the Otter. New York: Funk and Wagnalls, 1963. Grades 5-8.
Paul's father, a highly respected whaling captain, was lost at sea under mysterious circumstances, and Paul, now 15, has steadfastly believed that he is not dead. Born and bred to the sea, he longs to follow in his father's footsteps, but his mother refuses to sacrifice her only child to the deeps and apprentices him to a ship's chandler, a job in which he languishes. Unexpected support comes in the form of strange Tom, a crack harpooner who has been retired from the sea for fifteen years. He wants to make one last voyage, taking Paul with him as bunk mate, and he brooks no resistance. Under Tom's tutelage Paul learns the rigorous trade, but Tom will not divulge what he is seeking, only that there is a surprise at the end of every search. On a cannibalistic island in the South Seas their quest ends, but the surprise awaiting Paul at the end of the voyage when he is 18 is that he has returned in the very image of his father.

89. Weber, Lenora Mattingly. Meet the Malones. New York: Thomas Y. Crowell, 1943. Illus. by Gertrude Howe. Grades 7-9.

When Father accepts an assignment as war correspondent in Hawaii and their housekeeper is called to her daughter's home, the enterprising Malones agree to split the housework and the money saved doing it for their special projects: Mary Fred, 16, for her horse; Johnny, 15, for the typewriter he covets; and Beany, 13, for redecorating her room. But the work proves more arduous than they expect; sister Elizabeth, 19, arrives with her brand-new baby; and Mary Fred, flattered by the attention of the high school basketball star, finds it both expensive and time-consuming to be campus queen and social butterfly. Their problems appear to be solved when their stepgrandmother arrives, flourishing her golden wand like a fairy godmother, organizing the house and providing luxuries they have never known. Too late they learn that the wand has strings attached, and they have lost their pride and independence. All turn to dependable Mary Fred to take the initiative against Nonna. She is torn between her false social consciousness and her true social conscience but makes the right decision.

90. _____. Beany Malone. New York: Thomas Y. Crowell, 1948. Grades 7-9.

Sensible Beany, now 16 [see 89], shoulders the burdens of the whole madcap, motherless Malone menage: bringing sister Elizabeth's husband home from overseas and garnering coed Mary Fred a coveted bid from the Delts are but two of her campaigns. Her own personal life is complicated by the difficulty of attracting the boy she likes when he and his family are arch-enemies of the crusading Malones, and when the freckle cream she applies to her nose refuses to live up to expectations.

91. Wellman, Alice. The Wilderness Has Ears. New York: Harcourt, Brace, Jovanovich, 1975. Grades 7-9.

Fourteen-year-old Luti has grown up in the bush of Angola where her father, an American geologist, is employed. Because he is often on field trips, she is left in the care of the native Nduku who taught her to speak his dialect before she could speak English. When Nduku is grievously wounded by a leopard, he insists on returning to the healer and diviner in his Kimbutu village instead of to a modern hospital. She accompanies him but is scorned and spat upon for her sunburned white skin. Only the wise old diviner Onavita welcomes her and tends her burns after treating Nduku with her ancient remedies. When a sacred chameleon takes refuge in Luti's hair, the villagers believe that she harbors the spirit of an Old Soul and accord her reverence and respect. Marooned in the bush till her father comes for her, she shares the deprivation of the Long Dry that brings hunger-crazed hyenas to the very gates of the stockade, and participates in rites so old and sacred that sacrificial goats may not be eaten in the teeth of starvation. Ironically, the rain that ends the drought brings flash floods that threaten their holiest relics and Luti valiantly saves them.

92. Whitehead, Ruth. The Mother Tree. New York: Seabury Press, 1971. Illus. by Charles Robinson. Grades 5-7.

Tempe's mother's death from pneumonia changes her life radically, compelling her at 10 to be housekeeper for her father and brother Phil, 14, and nursemaid for her sister Laurie, 4, on their Texas farm at the turn of the century. The burden of responsibility, crowned by Phil's needling and jocular superiority, frays her young nerves to the breaking point. When Father and Phil depart to follow the harvest across the Southwest for extra cash, she leaps at the opportunity to stay with her grandparents which will enable her to be a little girl again. Under their gentle guidance and direction she still has chores to do and Laurie to look after, but it is not worrisome and there is time for carefree fun with her best chum and nearest neighbor. The three construct a playhouse in a lofty old mesquite which she calls the Mother Tree because its branches enfold her like a surrogate mother. When Father and Phil return at the end of the summer, she is reluctant to leave the comfort and security of Grandma's house and the sanctuary of her tree, but through Laurie's dependence on her she realizes that she has more strength than she supposed.

93. Williams, J. R. Oh, Susanna! New York: G. P. Putnam, 1963. Illus. by Albert Orbaan. Grades 7-9.

Susanna is 17 when her mother dies of consumption and her father decides to abandon his law practice in St. Louis at the close of the Civil War and become a homesteader in Kansas. While her brother helps Papa with the farm work, Susanna keeps house for the family in the dugout she despises on the boundless, windswept prairie, and has sole charge of her 7-year-old sister. Experienced neighbors help them till the soil and build a sod house, and Susanna soon finds that she has two beaux in a land where single men outnumber eligible women five to one: the suave, enigmatic schoolmaster, Joel Starret, and the rancher's son, Lin Camden, who has an axe to grind against his domineering father. When she encourages Lin to throw off his shackles and pursue the medical career he dreams of, she almost regrets it. She also experiences mixed emotions when her father wants to remarry. In the meantime stampedes, blizzards, malaria, Indians, buffalo, crop failure, and a pie supper enliven their days.

94. Wojciechowska, Maia. "Hey, What's Wrong with This One?" New York: Harper and Row, 1969. Illus. by Joan Sandin. Grades 3-4.

Three rambunctious motherless boys, Harley, Davidson, and little 7-year-old Mott inadvertently create a domestic crisis that causes the last of a succession of housekeepers to defect quite suddenly. Despairing of ever finding another acceptable one, the boys connive to supply their father with a perfect new wife--and themselves with the ideal mother. In a crowded supermarket Mott spots several possible candidates and causes considerable consternation and confusion for his father and a pretty young lady, but all's well that ends well, and the boys learn to cooperate and control themselves to please the lady who pleases all four Elliotts.

95. _____. Shadow of a Bull. New York: Atheneum, 1964. Illus. by Alvin Smith. Grades 5-7.

At 9, Manolo is aware that he bears a striking physical resemblance to his father, the legendary torero who put the town of Archangel on the map; that all its citizens expect him to emulate his father so that they can once more bask in reflected glory; and that he, Manolo, is a coward. The six aficionados and the Count who have supported him and his mother since his father's death by goring before his birth begin grooming him at this age for his inexorable tienta or public debut when he is 12, the age when his father began his ten-year career. Assisting the doctor who attends a novice matador who has been gored, he realizes that he wants to save lives, not take them. He promises his friend's brother Juan, who lives only to fight bulls and has an unerring instinct for it but who lacks financial support and opportunity, that he will intercede with the Count on his behalf. On the day of the corrida, he capes the bull for a few passes so as not to disgrace his mother, but hands the sword to Juan to demonstrate his brilliance in the denouement.

DIVORCE/DESERTION/SEPARATION

96. Alexander, Anne. To Live a Lie. New York: Atheneum, 1975. Illus. by Velma Ilsley. Grades 6-8.

    As 11-year-old Noel Jennifer, living with her father in a new town, begins junior high school she resolves to start a new life based on fiction: to repudiate the first name her mother derided; to tell everyone her mother is dead, not just getting divorced; and to make no friends and thus escape being hurt. Mom, she reasons, never wanted her in the first place, blamed the separation on her, caused her to lose her old friends, and deserted the children, forcing Jennifer to keep house for Dad, Ronnie, and little Linda, 5. The first two deceptions are surprisingly easy to carry off, but the decision to make no friends is difficult when everyone is so congenial. Only one girl goes out of her way to be disagreeable and inquisitive about her past, necessitating further obfuscations and compounding her misery. When Mom sends her a present for her twelfth birthday, she returns it unopened in mute indignation for all she has suffered on her account, instigating repercussions that end in total catharsis, new revelations, and renewed relationships based on a firm foundation.

97. Barnwell, Robinson. Shadow on the Water. New York: David McKay, 1967. Grades 6-8.

    Romantic, aristocratic, city-bred Mama and pragmatic, undemonstrative, country-bred Papa are bickering more and more acrimoniously over the disposition of money and other amenities, and communicating less and less, as the lingering Great Depression continues its siege of their South Carolina truck farm. Maternal grandmother Talbot prevails upon Mama to file for legal separation and move into her gracious Virginia mansion with the two younger children, Camden, 13, and Talbot, 6, much to the youngsters' dismay. Onetime tomboy Cammie adjusts to society life and the prospect of a new boyfriend better than brother Tal, but both miss home, father, and old friends. Beloved paternal grandfather Rutledge's death reunites the family, including attractive older sister Charlotte, 18, but a reconciliation between their parents seems hopeless until a posthumous letter is found from Grandpa to Mama telling her that

Papa has always loved her and needed her but is too stubborn to articulate it.

98. Bauer, Marion Dane. <u>Shelter from the Wind</u>. New York: Seabury Press, 1976. Grades 7-9.

For five years after her mother, hating the heat, dust and wind of the Oklahoma panhandle, ran off with another man, Stacy, now 12, and her father managed to live comfortably. Suddenly her father remarried and his new wife is about to bear their child. Fulminating with fury at Barbara's intruding presence and disgusted with the reproductive process, Stacy runs away to try to find her mother. Almost overcome by exposure and dehydration on the desert, she is led by pet dogs to the primitive abode of independent Old Ella who takes her in until she is ready to go on, teaching her self-reliance and responsibility. Through encounters with unsentimental Ella and Mr. Henderson who brings her supplies once a month, she vaguely recalls that her mother was an alcoholic who probably wouldn't want her even if she found her. The bittersweet whelping of Nimue's pups and its aftermath teach her the miracle of birth and the futility of hating. She decides to return to her father and stepmother but to visit Ella often.

99. Beatty, Patricia. <u>Me, California Perkins.</u> New York: William Morrow, 1968. Illus. by Liz Dauber. Grades 4-6.

Rapscallion Uncle Hiram inveigles peripatetic Pa to sell the Perkins' comfortable home in Sacramento in the 1880's and seek his fortune in the silver mining hamlet of Mojaveville on the desert, "the Creator's dumping ground," according to Mama, who has followed Pa resignedly from California to Oregon to Washington and back again, naming each of their three children, 13, 11, and 10, for the state in which he was born. This desolation, however, is too much for Mama who, with the children, moves into the only habitable domicile, a house made of whiskey bottles, leaving Pa to bunk in iniquitous bachelor diggings until he comes to his senses and is willing to move back to civilization. In the meantime she clerks in the mercantile store and with the collusion of the boarding house proprietress intrepidly conspires to bring law and order, running water, and a school teacher to town. Uncle Hiram almost sabotages the school by conducting the board of trustees like a marriage brokerage, but Mama prevails. Pa is stubborn too, and it isn't until the eldest daughter California is ready for high school that he recognizes her need for higher education and rejoins the family.

100. Blue, Rose. <u>A Month of Sundays</u>. New York: Franklin Watts, 1972. Illus. by Ted Lewin. Grades 3-5.

Ten-year-old Jeffrey returns from summer camp to learn that his parents are divorcing and that he and his mother are moving to New York City. He is disconsolate at leaving behind the suburban pursuits of Little League, biking and bowling, and dismayed at the melange of black, hispanic, and Jewish kids in his inner-city classroom. His Dad tries too hard to entertain him when he calls for him on Sundays, and his Mom is too tired when she gets home from work to cook his favorite dishes or even talk to him. A dynamic young teacher helps him adjust to his classmates and take an interest in school projects, but his other problems remain and he blames his mother for taking him from his father and being just a part-time Mom. He unburdens himself to a friend's mother who tactfully alerts Jeffrey's mother to the boy's feelings. Mom makes a special effort to contribute to the big block party, and Dad takes him to the park just to play catch as they used to do. When his old gang invites him back, he finds he is too busy making plans with his new friends.

101. Blume, Judy. <u>It's Not the End of the World</u>. Scarsdale, N.Y.: Bradbury Press, 1972. Grades 5-8.

Twelve-year-old Karen's paramount concern is to keep her separated parents from divorcing. She finds it totally inconceivable and unacceptable that her father should want to move away from home and live apart from her and her brother and sister. It is difficult to adjust to the change in daily routine, her mother's new job, the restaurant meals with Daddy, even though peace has been restored since her father's departure. She tries every wishful scheme to reunite her parents. Her brother runs away and precipitates a crisis she feels sure will reconcile them, but it only leads to more recrimination and spite. When she recognizes how futile her mission is and how miserable her parents make one another, acceptance becomes easier. The story weaves in a plug for Dr. Gardner's <u>The Boys and Girls Book about Divorce</u> [see Appendix, page 153].

102. Bradbury, Bianca. <u>Boy on the Run.</u> New York: Seabury Press, 1975. Grades 5-7.

Nick, 12, is a victim of smother love. His father is a remarried Washington VIP who is too busy to act paternal, and he lives with his over-anxious, self-indulgent mother in a prison of plush and perfume. Feeling cramped one day, he opens the apartment window and sends her cherished china crashing to the pavement of Manhattan below, is diagnosed as severely disturbed, and is remanded to his mother's punctilious psychiatrist. Seeing an opportunity to escape his gilded cage on his way to his grandmother's summer home, the astute boy turns some belongings into cash and adroitly engineers his bid for freedom on a neighboring resort island. There he dyes his hair to escape detection, buys a bike and survival gear, and enjoys a week of independence and adventure in which he acquires his first pet and first friend and learns that he doesn't need the tranquilizers Dr. Ada Carter-White so liberally dispenses. Arriving at his grandmother's house, he finds he can deal more effectively and incisively with both parents.

103. Cleaver, Vera, and Bill Cleaver. <u>Ellen Grae.</u> Philadelphia: J. B. Lippincott, 1967. Illus. by Ellen Raskin. Grades 5-6.

Eleven-year-old Ellen Grae Derryberry's divorced father sends her to town each September to spend the school year with the kindly McGruders whom she alternately amuses and exasperates with her tall tales and artful prevarications, particularly those with a preoccupation with violent or bizarre death. When the silent, simple swamp man Ira, who sells peanuts in the train depot, confides in her the gruesome circumstances of his parents' death, she harbors his secret until she becomes physically ill, knowing that the truth will mean either the penitentiary or the insane asylum for the harmless old man. Mrs. McGruder sends for Ellen Grae's parents who convince her that she has the moral obligation to make a clean breast of it. When the sheriff demonstrates condescending incredulity, she feels the mixed emotions of relief that Ira is saved and indignation over her besmirched honor, especially because her parents are angry. But her effervescent elan returns with Mrs. McGruder's warm affection, and she puts the unpleasantness out of her mind.

104. _____, and _____. Lady Ellen Grae.
Philadelphia: J. B. Lippincott, 1968. Illus. by Ellen
Raskin. Grades 5-6.
   Uninhibited Ellen Grae is enjoying the summer of
her eleventh year when her divorced parents decide to
turn her over to her priggish aunt to learn the social
graces and curb her fanciful stories. To forestall such
a fate she attempts to demonstrate that she can behave
like a lady on her own by donning false eyelashes and
getting a permanent, but her father is not fooled and
Aunt Eleanor and Cousin Laura duly arrive. Further
efforts to prove her command of etiquette only succeed
in nearly making a tomboy of Laura to Aunt Eleanor's
dismay, and she whisks both girls back to her ostenta-
tious home in Seattle. Elegant as it is, Ellen Grae cannot be acclimated to a life of cold and damp, sleeping
late, posh dinner parties, a maid to cook, clean and
iron, and worst of all, the onus of wearing gloves, ny-
lons, and a garter belt. There is method in her madness of being struck by the boom while out sailing, but
it almost doesn't succeed. It takes the outpouring of
affection from her many friends in her beloved Thicket,
Florida, to bring her home where she belongs, unspoiled.

105. Corcoran, Barbara. Axe-Time/Sword-Time. New York:
Atheneum, 1976. Grades 7-9.
   Struck in the head by a golf ball as a child, bright
18-year-old Elinor is left with a minor learning impairment that permits her to finish high school but not qualify for an Eastern Establishment college. Her posses-
sive, social-conscious mother will not acknowledge the
disability and insists that she take remedial courses to
pass College Board exams. Upon her parents' separation, her brother's enlistment in the armed services,
and her boyfriend's departure for Dartmouth, Elinor is
left to cope with her protective and domineering mother
alone. Mother objects strenuously when a sympathetic
teacher asks her to be a Civil Defense plane spotter in
the embryonic days of U. S. involvement in World War
II, but Elinor stands her ground. The ultimate test of
her self-reliance comes when her doctor father's formidable new fiancée challenges her to quit school and take
a job with the Navy in a defense plant, and she and her
mother almost stop speaking. Everyone else, however,
is proud of her initiative, especially her boyfriend, Jed,
now in uniform himself. Her handicap is not detrimental
at all.

98   The Single-Parent Family

106. _____. A Dance to Still Music. New York: Atheneum, 1974. Illus. by Charles Robinson. Grades 6-9.

    Left totally deaf from an untreated ear infection, 14-year-old Margaret is uprooted from her familiar New England hometown and brought to the Florida Keys by her waitress mother who is a conscious martyr to the cause of rearing Margaret alone, compounded by the burden of her handicap. Frightened and diffident in the hearing world where she is easy prey to danger and derision, Margaret alienates herself from human contact and even refuses to speak because she is afraid of making loud or peculiar noises as her deaf grandfather used to do. When her mother has the opportunity to remarry and the prospective husband offers to send her to a home for handicapped, anathema to Margaret, she decides to run away. Within a few miles she is providentially found by Josie, a motel chambermaid living in the isolation of a houseboat on the swampy Gulf coast. Josie accepts her as naturally as she does any of the wild creatures sharing the swamp, and Margaret becomes increasingly relaxed and finally begins to speak again, her pent up emotions tumbling out. The truant officers finally catch up with her, but through a teacher friend of Josie's she is able to enroll in an experimental day-school program at the university, and best of all, to continue living with Josie.

107. _____. This Is a Recording. New York: Atheneum, 1971. Illus. by Richard Cuffari. Grades 6-9.

    Marianne is an immature 14-year-old who resorts to hyperbole and occasional prevarication for effect. At the beginning of her sophomore year her parents send her to her grandmother in Montana, whom she has not seen since infancy, while they travel in Europe trying to mend an impaired marriage. Never having been west of the Hudson, Marianne is expecting cowboys and ranch houses. What she finds are her urbane grandmother's commodious Victorian mansion, civilized and educated Indians, hostile classmates reacting to her loftiness, and a bigoted, rapacious deputy sheriff and his son. Grandmother Katherine, who gave up an illustrious stage career to marry a rancher, comes out of retirement to give a vibrant performance that wins the respect of Marianne's classmates who then make friendly overtures to her. Marianne herself earns the respect of Katherine and her young Indian friend by saving his little brother's life. When her parents' marriage fails, Marianne is resentfully reluctant to return to Boston with her mother who seems so unfeeling, but she has acquired the maturity to handle it. She confides events and emotions to her tape recorder.

108. Donovan, John. I'll Get There. It Better Be Worth the Trip. New York: Harper and Row, 1969. Grades 7-9.
Following his parents' divorce when he was only five, Davy was sent to live with his grandmother who reared him with love and laughter along with his dachshund Fred in a small town near Boston. His complacent life is shattered eight years later by her unexpected death when he is uprooted and taken to New York to live in a tiny apartment with the selfish, unstable, alcoholic mother he scarcely knows. His shock and alienation are cushioned by his relationship with the adoring dog and a new friend he meets at his private school. Tentative sexual probings between the two boys result in a confrontation with Davy's erratic mother, following which the dog Fred is killed in a traffic accident. Seeking a scapegoat in his silent rage, Davy heaps guilt and shame upon himself, engulfs himself in sports, and shuns his friend. The tension explodes in a locker room fist fight which restores their friendship and Davy's self-respect. Unfortunate Fred's bathroom habits are described ad nauseum.

109. Duncan, Lois. A Gift of Magic. Boston: Little, Brown, 1971. Illus. by Arvis Stewart. Grades 5-8.
When her mother gets the nesting instinct, decides to divorce her war correspondent husband, and make a home for her three fledglings in Florida where she grew up, 12-year-old Nancy rebels. Her disapproval increases when her mother takes up where she left off with her childhood sweetheart, Mr. Duncan, who is now Nancy's junior high principal. Kirby, 13, has her gift of the dance to absorb her time and energy, and 9-year-old Brendon has a new friend plus his gift of music. Nancy inherited from her sage grandmother another special gift, that of ESP, but she tries to conceal it because she doesn't want to become a guinea pig. Her sister has an opportunity to study with a major ballet company, but Nancy doesn't want her to leave home. When Kirby falls and breaks her leg, Nancy believes she caused the accident by thought transference, but when Brendon embarks in a homemade boat, her clair-

voyance saves his life. Mr. Duncan's part in the rescue reveals his firm fiber, and her father's remarriage completes her catharsis and acceptance.

110. Dunnahoo, Terry. *Who Cares About Espie Sanchez?* New York: E. P. Dutton, 1975. Grades 7-9.

Esperanza means Hope, but Espie Sanchez has precious little of that when she is apprehended the third time for running away from her apathetic mother whose succession of degenerate boyfriends makes life untenable. Juvenile Hall seems inevitable until fate intervenes to place her in Mrs. Garcia's foster home, an alternative she accepts only because its minimum security affords the opportunity to run again. The religious atmosphere of the house and her roommate's involvement with police training through Law Enforcement Explorer Group (L. E. E. G.) are initially oppressive. Later she herself becomes a L. E. E. G. recruit as an excuse to get out of the house, but soon becomes seriously involved and determined to endure the rigorous training. When her brother dies of an overdose of drugs, she cooperates with the narcotics squad at grave personal risk to bring his supplier to justice. Against all odds but with the encouragement and faith of several, Espie triumphs over her hostility.

111. Ewing, Kathryn. *A Private Matter.* New York: Harcourt, Brace, Jovanovich, 1975. Illus. by Joan Sandin. Grades 4-5.

The people moving in next door are a friendly retired couple who have plenty of time to give 9-year-old Marcy the attention she lacks because her divorced father lives in California and her realtor mother works most of the time. Marcy tags along everywhere with Mr. Endicott as he potters about his house and garden, and he gives her little jobs to do to make her feel important. Soon she begins to fantasize in school compositions that he is her missing father. When her real father and his new wife want to take her on a weekend trip she tries unsuccessfully to circumvent it and is relieved to return to Mr. Endicott and the school project he is helping her with. But Mrs. Endicott's sudden death shatters their relationship. When he moves away Marcy experiences the same sense of loss and grief, and at the same time must adjust to the prospect of a new stepfather and the move to a new home.

112. Eyerly, Jeannette. <u>The World of Ellen March</u>. Philadelphia: J. B. Lippincott, 1964. Grades 7-9.

Sixteen-year-old Ellen's parents' divorce strikes her like a thunderbolt. Her mother takes her and her little sister to live in a small town in the Midwest where she attends public school and makes a friend but is afraid to join in group activities and cliques because of the imagined stigma of her broken home. She invents excuses for her father's absence while longing for the tangible evidence of his presence like the sound of his voice and the aroma of his pipe. Goaded by her friend and her own desperation to reunite her parents, she borrows the car and runs away with her sister to a secluded vacation home. Her strategy goes awry and terminates in an auto accident. Awakening in the hospital, she joyously believes she has effected a reconciliation when she sees her parents holding hands, only to learn later that they were humoring her, believing that she was in shock. Her disillusionment and demoralization are assuaged by an attractive male acquaintance who offers understanding, encouragement, and affection. An episode involving the death of a classmate's father subtly suggests that a divorced parent is better than a dead one.

113. Fitzhugh, Louise. <u>The Long Secret</u>. New York: Harper and Row, 1965. Illus. by the author. Grades 5-7.

Beth Ellen's blue-blooded grandmother, with whom she has lived in luxury for all of her 12 years, has tutored her to be a lady no matter what, and she has grown up timid, indolent and insipid. Her friend Harriet is of the opposite temperament, brash, abrasive and ambitious. She is determined to expose the perpetrator of the barbed, Biblical-sounding notes that have been surfacing around the summer colony. Beth Ellen is unprepared for the descension of the chic, brittle and sybaritic mother she hasn't seen in seven years and her vacuous, wealth-worshipping husband for whom she shed Beth Ellen's father. When she expresses a tentative desire to pursue an art career and be a productive member of society, they are first amused and then alarmed and decide to remove her from her grandmother's influence. She asserts herself histrionically at last, they lose interest, and her grandmother even condones her single breach of etiquette. Harriet finally finds her evidence, but the long secret has served its purpose.

114. Fox, Paula. How Many Miles to Babylon. New York: David White, 1967. Illus. by Paul Giovanopoulos. Grades 5-8.

When James' father deserted them, he and his mother went to live with his father's three aunts. Then his mother had to be hospitalized and was lost to him also. The introverted boy seeks desperately to find her. One day he spies a shiny dime store ring he takes as an omen that today he will see her. Playing truant, he goes to the basement of a derelict house in his New York slum where he fantasizes that his mother is an African queen and he communes with her. The house is also the headquarters of a tough teenage ring of dog thieves who surprise him and under duress put him to work for them. That night he makes a harrowing and abortive attempt to escape them in the dark, deserted funhouse at Coney Island. Later he manages to elude the hoodlums, return the dog he took, and make his way home--where his mother is awaiting him.

115. _____. Blowfish Live in the Sea. Englewood Cliffs, N.J.: Bradbury Press, 1970. Grades 6-9.

Written from his 12-year-old half sister Carrie's viewpoint, this is the story of 18-year-old Ben who has lived with his mother and stepfather since his parents' divorce and who, a year earlier, dropped out and turned off, his long hair and lassitude becoming a bone of contention between him and his stepfather. Carrie, however, adores and defends him, and when his real father, a purportedly prosperous Arizona rancher, suddenly surfaces in Boston and wants to see him, he asks Carrie to accompany him. The bon vivant father turns out to be nothing but a seedy, drunken bum with a touch of engaging elegance living in a flophouse hotel. Ben's decision to remain in Boston and rehabilitate his father gives him the direction he needs in life, but Carrie realizes that he has grown up and left her behind. The present he leaves her explains the significance of his cryptic slogan, "Blowfish live in the sea."

116. Goff, Beth. Where Is Daddy? The Story of a Divorce. Boston: Beacon Press, 1969. Illus. by Susan Perl. Grades K-2.

Janeydear loved to play with Daddy and Funny the dog, but sometimes Daddy would scold when she wanted to play and made too much noise, and one day he wasn't there at all and Mommy didn't know when he was returning. Janey wonders if he is angry with her, but when he does come back and takes her to the beach all by herself, she thinks everything is going to be fine because she doesn't understand the word divorce. That evening her parents quarrel and Daddy goes away again, promising that he will always be her daddy. Janey and Mommy go to live with Grandma who is strict about dogs. Then Mommy gets a job and Janey is more lonely, angry and bewildered than before. When she vents her frustrations on Funny, the adults finally recognize her inarticulate fears and give her the attention and reassurance she needs, and Daddy comes to take her to the zoo.

117. Greene, Constance C. A Girl Called Al. New York: Viking Press, 1969. Illus. by Byron Barton. Grades 4-6.

When Al first moves to Apartment 14C she is a conscious nonconformist, compensating for her broken home. Her chic, svelte mother works all day and dates most evenings, and her father sends her plenty of money but never writes, calls or visits. Left to her own devices the lonely and intense seventh-grader gorges herself to obesity, wears a homely hairstyle, and hates being called Alexandra. She and the amusingly ingenuous narrator of the story, a girl who lives down the hall and attends the same class, become firm friends. With the tactful help of the inimitable building superintendent, Mr. Richards, a retired bartender and armchair philosopher, Al begins to think positively about herself, make the best of the situation, and improve her appearance. Mr. Richards' untimely death sobers and matures both girls, but memories of shared camaraderie buoy their spirits once more.

118. _____. I Know You, Al. New York: Viking Press, 1975. Illus. by Byron Barton. Grades 5-7.

At 13, Al is tired of waiting [see 117] --waiting to be attractive, waiting to be popular, waiting to get her period. An unexpected telephone call from the father she hasn't seen in six years forestalls her adolescent maunderings but plunges her into a sea of ambivalence. Her father invites her to attend his wedding and meet his new family, and while she is delirious about seeing him and meeting her stepbrothers, she is nervous about making a good impression and is especially resentful that her father could just walk out of her and her

mother's lives and now just as coolly reenter. Her
fears are abolished at the wedding, she takes compassion
on her father, and anticlimactically gets her period.
For a nonconformist she is pretty predictable to her
bosom buddy who acts as foil for Al's wit and records
her trials and tribulations in droll prose.

119. Heide, Florence Parry. When the Sad One Comes to Stay. Philadelphia: J. B. Lippincott, 1975. Grades 5-7.

Sara's mother Sally with whom she has come to live
is a successful, sophisticated, stylish, snobbish social
climber who is trying to remake Sara in her own image.
When Sally collected her from her father, a junk dealer,
she discarded her old shabby clothes and toys, bought
her new expensive ones, deposited her and her finery
in a modern decorator apartment at a good address,
and told her to make friends among the pampered daughters of privilege and influence. Instead, the lonely girl
befriends an equally lonely, impoverished, uneducated
old woman who encourages her to delve into her fading
memory for reminiscences of her happy, carefree life
with her fun-loving father and half brother. Sally, believing that the past should be obliterated, gets an unlisted telephone number when Sara's father tries to get
in touch with her. The repressed and beleaguered
child's last opportunity to assert herself comes when
Sally decides to go to New York for a few days. Sara
follows the course of least resistance.

120. Holland, Isabelle. Heads You Win; Tails I Lose. Philadelphia: J. B. Lippincott, 1973. Grades 7-9.

An undemonstrative, reactionary father with a cruel
streak and a progressive, brutally frank mother with a
fault-finding bent create a volatile environment for overweight 15-year-old Melissa who is already agonizing
over her inability to attract the boy she likes. The
battered ball in a vicious game of her parents, she
finally rebels against their chronic withering criticism
and exhorts them to get divorced. After her father's
departure, her mother resorts to alcohol in her self-pity, and Melissa resorts to filching her mother's diet
pills to lose weight and her sleeping tablets to offset
the effect of the amphetamines. The weight loss is
dramatic, but she finally "trips out" at rehearsal for a
school play and everything "hits the fan." A compassionate teacher and a perceptive boy, her only friends,

help her tie the tattered ends and grasp the reins of her own life while effecting a reconciliation with her father and coping maturely with her mother until she can go her independent adult way when she turns 18.

121. Johnson, Annabel, and Edgar Johnson. <u>The Grizzly.</u> New York: Harper and Row, 1964. Illus. by Gilbert Riswold. Grades 5-8.

Sensitive and artistic like his mother with whom he lives, David is alarmed when his rugged outdoorsman father Mark arrives to take him camping at a remote wilderness site. His father's motive is to make a man of him, but David, bolstered by recurring nightmares, fears that Mark will harm him physically or abandon him to test his mettle. Mark, however, saves him when a savage mother grizzly protecting her cubs attacks him, then turns to maul Mark. The stark question of survival necessitates David's trust and cooperation, and gradually he dispels his diffidence and masters new skills. At the same time, his father acknowledges that his methods of imparting maturation may have been clumsy in his thinly veiled statement, "Not all animals are born to be good fathers." The story closes with David's unrealistic hope that his parents will be reconciled.

122. Kerr, M. E. <u>Love Is a Missing Person.</u> New York: Harper and Row, 1975. Grades 8-9.

When their parents divorced, Daddy chose vibrant individualist daughter Chicago to live in New York with him, while introverted Suzy remained with her mother. Suddenly Chicago, now 17, a spoiled, self-styled revolutionary, returns and proposes that she and Suzy, 15, change places. Her reason soon becomes obvious when their father marries a sleazy redhead young enough to be his daughter, in effect usurping Chicago's position. The two sisters with such dichotomous personalities try living together in armed truce at their mother's lavish beach estate, the one quietly pursuing library volunteer work, the other ostentatiously and quixotically organizing her revolution to end oppression of minorities and equalize the classes while paradoxically demanding and taking for granted the appurtenances of wealth. When Chicago proselytizes the class valedictorian, a black, and woos him from his former sweetheart, Suzy's best friend, she triggers a tragedy that eventually drives them underground. Suzy can't begin to comprehend her sister but she does develop compassion.

123. Klein, Norma. It's Not What You Expect. New York: Pantheon, 1973. Grades 7-9.

  The summer that Dad feels trapped and unfulfilled and moves to an apartment in New York looms long and bleak to 14-year-old twins Carla and Oliver and their Mom until Oliver, an haute cuisine chef, hatches a scheme to open an expensive restaurant in a neighbor's home, run entirely by the kids and their friends in their sleepy corner of exurbia. Their venture is supremely successful, and the work involved makes the months fly, yet affords Carla some private moments for pondering the perplexities of life. Unlike her brother who is a pragmatist and almost as relaxed and unaffected as Mom, Carla is idealistic and often depressed and pessimistic over the exigencies of existence, including divorce. She would like to live according to a preconceived plan, but Oliver submits that life is fraught with unforeseen pitfalls. As if to prove his point, their 18-year-old brother's girlfriend becomes pregnant and has an abortion. At the end of the summer, his restlessness allayed, Dad returns to his family.

124. _____. Taking Sides. New York: Pantheon, 1974. Grades 5-8.

  A year in the life of 12-year-old Nell whose parents are divorced has its ups and downs, its introspections and insights. Being sent from her mother's place in the country to Dad's apartment in the city is not onerous, because she secretly prefers her father and can still visit her working mother on weekends. Sharing a room with her kid brother who wets the bed, accepting her father's girlfriend, and coping with the dilemma of divided holidays require more difficult adjustments. Her father's sudden heart attack reverses the plan and forces another adaptation. Interludes with her first boyfriend and heart-to-heart confidences with her best girlfriend are part of any girl's young teen experience.

125. _____. What It's All About. New York: Dial Press, 1975. Grades 6-8.

  Oriental on her father's side and Jewish on her mother's, 11-year-old Bernadette lives in New York with her mother and her mother's new husband Gabe. The family grows with the adoption of Suzu, a Vietnamese orphan who adores Bernie but can be temperamental. Soon Gabe loses his job, grows surly, abusive and belligerent, and finally disappears. In the meantime, Bernie's father remarries and she is invited to the wedding where she learns that the new wife, Peggy, is already seven months' pregnant. They offer her a home with them when they hear of her unstable homelife and her mother's second divorce, but she declines, knowing she'd miss her mother and Suzu. After the baby is born, her father and Peggy invite the three of them to visit. After a pleasant vacation in California they return to New York to discover that Gabe has returned with his daughter by his first marriage. He has a new girlfriend, but they all remain amicable and Bernie becomes friendly with Gabe's daughter. Perplexed by conflicting loyalties, Bernie vows she will never marry, but her sagacious grandmother (who has just remarried at 62) tells her, "You can like a lot of people, but you can only love a few."

126. Lexau, Joan M. Emily and the Klunky Baby and the Next-Door Dog. New York: Dial Press, 1972. Illus. by Martha Alexander. Grades 2-3.

The last time there was new snow, Emily and her mother made a snowman together, but since her parents' divorce Mama is always too busy to play. Today she is doing income tax, and Emily must entertain the klunky old baby. But all their games are too noisy, and a preoccupied Mama banishes them to play outdoors. Full of self-pity, Emily resolves to run away to Dad's apartment. But the baby falls off the sled and cries, the next-door dog follows them, and worst of all, she becomes hopelessly lost turning corners. Following the dog, they complete the circuit of the block and miraculously find themselves in front of their own house with Mama cheerfully waving from the window, unaware of the tense drama and averted disaster. She has finished the taxes and is ready for another project with which Emily can help.

127. _____. Me Day. New York: Dial Press, 1971. Illus. by Robert Weaver. Grades K-2.

Rafer awakens on the morning of his birthday feeling the world is his oyster. Gradually he becomes preoccupied with thoughts of his divorced father and the letter he always receives from him on his birthday. Soon his mood turns morose after the mailman comes and goes with no missive for him. A mysterious telephone message sends him on a grudging errand to the fruit store--until he spies his father waiting for him on the street corner. "Did you undivorce me?" Rafer asks. Daddy replies slowly, "Look, your mother and me are divorced. Not you kids. No way! You and me are tight, buddy. Together like glue, O. K. ?" "O. K., Daddy," Rafer says. His world is rosy again.

128. Lisker, Sonia O., and Leigh Dean. <u>Two Special Cards</u>. New York: Harcourt, Brace, Jovanovich, 1976. Illus. by Sonia O. Lisker. Grades 1-3.

Hazel Cooper, 7, thinks getting a divorce is miserable because all her parents do is yell and fight. She wishes her 3-year-old brother were old enough to talk to. Then one night her father packs and moves out. Life is much more peaceful, but she wonders if Daddy is ever coming back and whether Mom will leave, too. Then Daddy calls and arranges to pick up her and Billy to stay overnight with him in his new apartment in the city. After a wonderful weekend Hazel decides divorce isn't so bad because now she has two happy homes. When they return, they go shopping for cards for Grandma's birthday, and Hazel wants to get one for Mom and Daddy, too, expressing her love for them. She can't find one about getting divorced, so she makes one of her own and cuts it in half for her two special parents.

129. Mann, Peggy. <u>My Dad Lives in a Downtown Hotel</u>. Garden City, N.Y.: Doubleday, 1973. Illus. by Richard Cuffari. Grades 4-5.

When Joey's father storms out of the apartment one night and doesn't return, and his mother is in tears next morning at breakfast, Joey knows it must be his fault. After school he takes the bus to his father's office and presents him with a list of resolutions for being a better son if only his dad will return home. Dad explains that the only good part of their marriage was having Joey and the bad was not Joey's fault. Then he arranges to take him to the circus. But his mom is still distressed, and Joey hates Dad for hurting her. At the circus Dad overcompensates by buying him too many sweets and he is sick, but still it is fun because Dad never had time to take him places before. Dad takes the old TV but replaces it with a color set, and the noise of it helps fill the void in the lonesome evenings. When he discovers that 53 kids on the block have no father living at home, he decides to form a secret club and at last regains a sense of belonging.

130. Mazer, Harry. <u>Guy Lenny.</u> New York: Delacorte Press, 1971. Grades 6-9.

   Twelve-year-old Guy and his father have lived companionably since his parents' divorce many years earlier until the advent of Emily who, to Guy, constitutes the proverbial "crowd," and he doesn't attempt to mask his sentiments. Then the mother he doesn't remember arrives with her husband and starts making maternal overtures to him, compounding his confusion and resentment. When he learns that his father has sent for his mother and asked her to make a home for Guy so he can marry Emily and make a life of his own, Guy feels bitter and betrayed. In his rage and self-pity he wishes he would die but then reasons that death might be lonesome and uncomfortable. He realizes that he can survive on the strength of his individuality, no matter which parent he decides to live with. Threaded through the theme are encounters with the neighborhood punk and Guy's first sexual stirrings.

131. Neville, Emily Cheney. <u>Garden of Broken Glass.</u> New York: Delacorte Press, 1975. Grades 7-8.

   White, 13-year-old Brian leads a tangential existence with three black classmates in a St. Louis slum, brooding and drifting in a self-imposed vacuum because his problem seems so hopeless and insurmountable: an alcoholic mother who makes homelife intolerable with her open favoritism for his younger brother. He can't leave home as his dimly recollected father did, and his resentment aggravates the situation. In his loneliness and diffidence, he seeks the companionship of a stray dog. But his would-be human friends have difficulties, too, and one-by-one seek him for solace: Dwayne when his coolness gets him in trouble with housing project toughs and his father grounds him; Fat Martha when she fears she may be pregnant. As the long, emotionally turbulent summer closes, Brian's older sister brutally confronts him with the fact that their mother's illness is permanent and they must learn to cope with it. Martha and Dwayne, with his girlfriend Melvita, accept him into their circle.

132. Newfield, Marcia. <u>A Book for Jodan.</u> New York: Atheneum, 1975. Illus. by Diane de Groat. Grades 2-4.

   The first eight years of Jodan's life overflow with the camaraderie of family togetherness and mutual cooperation. When she is 9 her parents begin arguing.

Jodan isn't sure which is worse--the unhappy silences or the noisy quarrels. Then her mother announces their separation, and she and Jodan move back to California. Her father writes to her, but she misses their bedtime conversations and hugs, and eventually begins to forget what he looks like. When she visits him at Easter vacation, he gives her a special looseleaf scrapbook he has been creating for her when she is lonesome for him. It contains a potpourri of remembrances, incidents, anecdotes, advice and activities, as well as old photos.
Best of all, this intimate communion between father and daughter can be supplemented as time goes on and is physical evidence of his love. She decides to make one for him.

133. Norris, Gunilla B. Lillan. New York: Atheneum, 1968. Illus. by Nancie Swanberg. Grades 5-6.

Lillan was the pet name given to 10-year-old Ingalill by her extravagant Papa before he deserted her and Mama a year ago, and now Lillan is assailed by doubts that if her father and mother could stop loving one another, it follows that her mother might also stop loving her. To make ends meet in post-war Sweden, Mama must rent out the best rooms in the house and take a job, leaving her little time and energy for companionship with Lillan. When her mother begins keeping steady company with a man she met at work, Lillan's fears are intensified. In her shame over the divorce, she is reluctant to go to school and make friends but eventually overcomes that stigma. The tug of war at home for her mother's affections continues, however, and in her anxiety she begins taking things that don't belong to her just for the feeling of possession. But Jon proves to be a gentle and understanding compadre, and he and Mama gradually allay her fears. Her eleventh birthday becomes a real family occasion, and she decides to use her real name, relegating thoughts of Papa to childhood memories.

134. Peck, Richard. Don't Look and It Won't Hurt. New York: Holt, Rinehart and Winston, 1972. Grades 6-9.

Fifteen-year-old Carol narrates the saga of the unhappy homelife of the Patterson family whose father deserted them when her younger sister, now 9, was a baby and whose shrewish mother barely supports them in a grim hand-to-mouth existence by working the night shift at a diner. Carol is the sensible one, though gawky, who earns good grades and shoulders responsibility. Her older sister, 17, is uncontrollable, runs with a fast crowd, eventually gets into trouble, and must go away to a home for unwed mothers, whereupon their mother transfers her suspicions to Carol. Carol's maturity, insight, and decisiveness save the family from total disintegration and restore a modicum of peace and hope.

135. Perl, Lila. The Telltale Summer of Tina C. New York: Seabury Press, 1975. Grades 6-7.
   Since their parents' divorce, Tina, 12, and Arthur, 9, have remained with their father in their expensive Long Island suburb. Now their less conventional mother and her new husband Peter have returned to New York where they have taken an apartment and want the children to spend the summer. Arthur is delighted, but Tina, who is resistant to her mother's new husband and lifestyle, wants to remain at home with her friends, the Saturday Sad Souls Club. The SSSC was formed as a self-help beauty club for girls with problems (Tina is a lanky string bean with a nervous habit of wrinkling her nose when self-conscious), but the induction of a new member causes strife and Tina drops out. She decides to spend the remainder of the summer with her mother and Peter after all. In the city she meets her first boyfriend, discovers that personal appearances are not nearly as important as she thought, and comes to like Peter. She returns home more self-confident and learns that her father has reconsidered his own remarriage plans.

136. Pfeffer, Susan Beth. The Beauty Queen. Garden City, N.Y.: Doubleday, 1974. Grades 7-9.
   Impelled by an overbearing mother seeking her own wish fulfillment, gorgeous Kit Carson half-heartedly enters a local beauty pageant, determined to lose. Her competitive spirit prevails, however, and she wins. Her jubilant mother, basking in reflected glory, insists that she continue to the county, state and national finals, thwarting 18-year-old Kit's personal desire to pursue an acting career. After winning the county contest, she is nagged by the fear that her looks, not her talent, have been responsible for her success in the theatre. Philosophically she resigns herself to the knowledge that while her dramatic ability is genuine, her physical attributes afford a distinct advantage. With equanimity

she cuts the maternal apron strings, abdicates her title, and strikes out to test her talent with a new acting company.

137. _____. Marly the Kid. Garden City, N. Y.: Doubleday, 1975. Grades 7-9.

At 15, Marly Carson also runs away from her harridan of a mother [see 136] to live with her father and his new wife, and gradually begins to emerge from the cocoon she has woven about her in self-defense. She makes her first best friend, gets a crush on her English teacher who is not only an outstanding instructor but looks like Robert Redford as well, and gets suspended for daring to retort when her sarcastic, chauvinistic history teacher calls her (accurately) "plain, plump and pimply." Her bluff father, diplomatic stepmother, and laudatory schoolmates rally to her defense, and her self-confidence is replete.

138. Platt, Kin. The Boy Who Could Make Himself Disappear. Philadelphia: Chilton, 1968. Grades 6-9.

Ignored by his preoccupied Hollywood producer father and verbally brutalized by his self-centered artist mother, Roger developed a speech impediment which grows more acute as he gets older and more self-conscious. It is aggravated when his parents divorce when he is 12 and his mother takes him to New York to live, where a sarcastic teacher at his private school ridicules him, and his mother's abuse grows more vitriolic. But others accept and befriend him: the glamorous model who lives in the penthouse, her French boyfriend who once overcame his own vocal impairment, the crippled girl in the opposite wing who takes no quarter, and above all, Miss Clemm, the psychiatrist and speech therapist at school. With her encouragement he makes such dramatic progress that he tries to share the good news with his father by telephone, only to receive another rebuff. It is enough to send the unwanted, unloved boy into schizophrenic withdrawal and eventually into a regressive, infantile autistic state. With the aid of Miss Clemm and the Frenchman he begins the long road to recovery.

139. _____. Chloris and the Creeps. Philadelphia: Chilton, 1973. Grades 5-7.

Chloris, 11, and Jenny, 8, can scarcely remember their profligate, philandering father who divorced their mother six years before and committed suicide three years later. When their mother starts dating other men (the creeps) and contemplates remarriage, the girls are not sure they need a new father; Jenny keeps an open mind, while Chloris is adamantly opposed to any change in the status quo. She becomes chief proselytizer in the cult to deify her father of which her paternal grandmother is high priestess. When their mother decides to marry Fidel Mancha, a Chicano sculptor, Chloris reacts with stony negativism and open hostility, blackballing Fidel's bid for legal adoption. When her mother erupts in anger and exasperation, Chloris goes on a rampage of deliberate destruction, climaxing in the torching of Fidel's studio. Psychiatry fails to overcome her stubborn resistance, but Fidel's saintly forbearance, wisdom and compassion finally triumph.

140. _____. Chloris and the Freaks. Scarsdale, N. Y.: Bradbury Press, 1975. Grades 5-8.

Chloris, now 14 [see 139], resurrects her father's spirit and perniciously plots her mother's divorce from Fidel. Jenny, 12, who adores Fidel, consults the stars to try to reverse the portent, perceiving that being dubbed a freak depends largely on whether Chloris is jealous of someone. But Jenny's astrological machinations and Fidel's pontifical patience fail to curb her mother's restlessness, and she takes up with a business associate while Fidel is off at a showing of his sculpture. Chloris appears receptive to this one to hasten her mother's decision, and it is Jenny's turn to play devil's advocate. But when the divorce plans are announced, Chloris unmasks her single-minded vituperation for all the men in her mother's life except her own father, taking grim satisfaction in making others unhappy to gain her perverse ends. Jenny is no more successful in preventing her teacher's and her best friend's parents' divorce. They both feel wretched.

141. Sachs, Marilynn. The Bears' House. Garden City, N. Y.: Doubleday, 1971. Illus. by Louis Glanzman. Grades 5-6.

After her father's desertion and her mother's ensuing mental illness, 10-year-old Fran Ellen has only two things to live for: her beloved baby sister for whom she has sole responsibility, and the Three Bears' dollhouse in her classroom into which she escapes in fantasy when the pressures of stark reality overwhelm her. Tormented by siblings and peers alike, she lives a life of deception, trying to keep the family intact. Her world dissolves when the baby becomes ill and a discerning teacher discovers their tragic plight. Left with only the dollhouse family (a gift from her teacher for breaking her thumb-sucking habit) for solace, acceptance and love, her daydreams supply the rationalization for giving up her precious baby: that the baby needs proper care or she will die. In the end, retreat into her fantasy family becomes her only defense, her only tolerable recourse.

142. Slote, Alfred. <u>Matt Gargan's Boy.</u> Philadelphia: J. B. Lippincott, 1975. Grades 5-6.

Danny's parents were divorced because his Mom hated being a "baseball widow," married to a major league player, but now his father is on the verge of retirement and Danny, 11, hopes he will return to their small town and the three of them will take up where they left off. When his mother starts seeing a man whose daughter wants to join his Little League team, he reasons that the two would be attending games together and might get serious about one another, so he heads the delegation to deliver the ultimatum that they want no girls on their team. Susie is given a tryout anyway and passes handily. The other boys accept her but Danny quits the team. He is jolted when his mother attends the next game without him and calls his Dad for advice, only to discover that he is planning to remarry. His defenses in tatters, he surrenders to the inevitable, but is still proud to be Matt Gargan's son.

143. Smith, Doris Buchanan. <u>Tough Chauncey.</u> New York: William Morrow, 1974. <u>Illus. by Michael Eagle.</u> Grades 7-8.

Thirteen-year-old Chauncey would never hurt an animal, only people, because people hurt him. His thrice-divorced mother whom he adores can't make a home for him because of her succession of boyfriends, so he lives with his grandparents who inflict brutality in the guise of stern moral guidance. His grandfather believes it is sinful to attend movies but cold-bloodedly shoots kittens and beats the boy and locks him in the closet when he is ten minutes late from school. Calculatedly Chauncey has become the toughest, meanest kid in his Georgia town, cutting a swath of malicious mischief and destruction. In a last-ditch effort to live with his mother, he is badly hurt jumping from a train and returned to his grandparents on crutches. When his grandfather tries to shoot his last defenseless kitten, he has no recourse but to run away, despite his incapacitation. He is aided by his erstwhile arch-enemy and fellow scapegrace, a black, who tells him of his own intolerable homelife and suggests a foster home as an alternative in Chauncey's bid to make good.

144. Snyder, Anna. *First Step*. New York: Holt, Rinehart and Winston, 1975. Grades 7-9.

It is common knowledge that Cindy Stott's mother is an alcoholic, but Cindy continues to protect and defend her and finally withdraws from her friends in an attempt to avoid hurt and humiliation. When she commands the lead in the high school play and the leading man, Mitch, along with it, a jealous cast member cruelly baits Cindy about her mother's drinking problem, and the defensive girl rises to it with the desired effect every time. Mitch discloses that his parents are both alcoholics and invites her to Alateen meetings, but she remains skeptical. When her mother injures her younger brother in alcoholic anger, she calls her father in New York to ask if he will send for them, but while he is willing to send support payments, he makes it clear that he wants no further commitments. On opening night her mother makes a sensational performance of her own, eclipsing Cindy's stellar one and plunging her to a nadir of mortification, at last receptive to the ministrations of Alateen and loyal, long-suffering Mitch.

145. Snyder, Zilpha Keatley. *Eyes in the Fishbowl*. New York: Atheneum, 1968. Illus. by Alton Raible. Grades 5-7.

Fourteen-year-old Dion is vaguely dissatisfied with his impecunious father's lethargic lifestyle after his mother left, and wants to pursue for himself the conventional materialistic life. Between his many part-time jobs he slips into the city's most sumptuous department store to savor the aura of luxury it exudes. One day he sees an exotic girl there with enigmatic dark eyes, and when he is accidentally locked in the store after closing hours he discovers that she and some unseen companions live there and are responsible for ghostly occurrences and unexplained voices that are unnerving for customers and employees alike. It is only after he has developed a close attachment to Sara that he learns she and her friends are spirits who have been materialized there by an elderly psychic, and he is in mortal jeopardy of joining them. After Sara's departure and the failure of the store, Dion realizes his father would feel stifled in a permanent, paying position, renews his latent interest in music, and savors success as part of a dance combo.

146. Stolz, Mary. Leap Before You Look. New York: Harper and Row, 1972. Grades 8-9.

At Christmas, 14-year-old Janine reviews the events of the past year: the trivial and profound discussions with family and friends, the eventful bus trips to and from school, the fateful slumber party when she got her first period, but most of all the events surrounding her parents' divorce and the changes it effected in all their lives. Although her parents are a study in contrasts and discord, her mother intellectual and impassive, her father warm and responsive, she is totally unprepared for their split and reacts with acrimonious recrimination. Her father quickly remarries, and she and her mother and brother Goya, 5, go to live with the grandmother she considers a snob who belittles her father's dentistry practice. While she never develops a closer relationship with her mother, she comes to appreciate her grandmother more. Time dulls her rancor, as does her first boyfriend, and on Christmas Day she finally forgives her absent father.

147. Thomas, Ianthe. Eliza's Daddy. New York: Harcourt, Brace, Jovanovich, 1976. Illus. by Moneta Barnett. Grades K-2.

Eliza's parents are divorced and her father has remarried. He lives across town with his wife, baby and stepdaughter who is about Eliza's age, but he spends every Saturday with Eliza. One night she has a dream that her father's stepdaughter is an accomplished horsewoman, beautiful and smart, a "Wonderful Angel Daughter." The next Saturday when Daddy asks her what she wants to do, she vows to ask him to take her to his new house and meet his new family, but she loses her nerve. The following week, however, she is resolute and finds that her stepsister is an ordinary, friendly sort of girl like she is. Daddy takes them pony riding together.

148. Wagner, Jane. J. T. New York: Van Nostrand Reinhold, 1969. Illus. by Gordon Parks, Jr. Grades 2-4.

J. T. Gamble steals a radio from a parked car

because he knows he won't get one for Christmas but
has to run for his life to escape Claymore and Boomer,
bigger bullies who are also after the radio. His mother
accuses him of "turnin' bad" like the father who deserted
them. Among the rubble of a razed tenement he finds
a starving, injured cat for which he makes an elaborate
shelter out of junk, cutting school to care for his pet
and scrounging food for it by charging it to his mother's
account until she discovers and puts an end to it. Boomer and Claymore find the cat's sanctuary, and the terrified cat, Bones, runs into the path of a car and is killed.
The inconsolable boy is comforted by the wisdom of his
grandmother who also helps his mother to understand
him better. For Christmas the grocer brings him a
stray kitten which his mother allows him to keep. More
mature and secure, he returns the radio, faces down
Boomer and Claymore, asks the grocer for a job, and
returns to school.

149. Wolitzer, Hilma. Out of Love. New York: Farrar, Straus and Girous, 1976. Grades 7-8.
   Reading her father's old love letters to her mother,
13-year-old Teddy wishes dowdy Mother would lose
weight and take an interest in clothes and cosmetics to
lure Daddy away from his glamorous new wife Shelley,
who is the Enemy even if she does seem nice. Her
sister Karen, 11, doesn't share her resentment but has
a different campaign, to make Mother stop smoking.
Teddy's attitude toward Shelley thaws when she asks
Shelley's advice on beauty matters and gets a flattering
haircut, but it isn't until Shelley and Teddy's father announce that they are expecting a baby that her hopes for
repairing the family rift go aglimmering. She learns
that beauty is in the eye of the beholder, and if she
turns out to be like her mother it won't be half bad.
She has learned to accept what she cannot change, while
her best friend Maya has valiantly changed a situation
she cannot accept.

150. Zolotow, Charlotte. A Father Like That. New York: Harper and Row, 1971. Illus. by Ben Shecter. Grades K-2.
   "I wish I had a father. But my father went away
before I was born. I say to my mother, you know what
he'd be like? 'What?' she says.'" Thus a little boy
launches into a description of his fabulous fantasy father
who plays checkers with him, helps around the house,

goes to PTA meetings, comforts him, disciplines him gently, understands and supports him. Mother replies, "I like the kind of father you're talking about. And in case he never comes, just remember when you grow up, you can be a father like that yourself!"

ORPHAN WITH SINGLE GUARDIAN

151. Alexander, Anne. **Trouble on Treat Street.** New York: Atheneum, 1974. Illus. by John Jones. Grades 5-7.
     Clem gets off to an inauspicious start when he moves to the San Francisco ghetto with his grandmother after the accidental death of his parents. Manolo, a boy his age, lives in the same building but takes an instant dislike to Clem simply because Clem's black, not Chicano like Manolo. In school they are paired together in fifth grade but maintain their unsheathed hostility until a gang of older toughs of mixed race tries to play the two against each other. Just as they achieve one another's trust and friendship, Clem's grandmother and Manolo's mother each jump to the erroneous conclusion that the other boy is a bad influence on hers through circumstantial evidence. Only after Clem's Granny saves the life of Manolo's baby brother does the true story unfold, and Mrs. Gomez in gratitude invites the newcomers to a party and Clem stands up to the bullies.

152. Bawden, Nina. **The Witch's Daughter.** Philadelphia: J. B. Lippincott, 1966. Grades 5-8.
     Orphaned in infancy, 11-year-old Perdita has been reared by kind, elderly Annie on a tiny island off the coast of Scotland where she has run as free and wild as the wind and grown as shy and stunted as the flowers in their rocky crevices. Annie acts as housekeeper for the enigmatic Mr. Smith who does not allow Perdita to attend school or make friends, hence she is taunted and feared as a witch by the other island children. When the steamer brings a vacationing family and a mysterious stranger to Skua, Perdita finds her first friends in blind Janey and her imaginative brother Tim. The children pool their extraordinary capabilities to solve an almost perfect crime and save one another from the brink of disaster. Tim's inquisitive mind provides the impetus, Perdita's ESP rescues Tim from peril, but Janey who has developed acute senses of touch and hearing emerges as the heroine when the trio is stranded in the Stygian depths of a cave by the ring of jewel thieves. Mr. Smith has been kind to Perdita in his clumsy way, and when his complicity is revealed, she warns him to escape and grieves when he loses his life in the attempt.

Her new friends promise to return, and in the meantime she will start school.

153. Bellairs, John. <u>The Figure in the Shadows</u>. New York: Dial Press, 1975. Illus. by Mercer Mayer. Grades 5-7.

When chubby, timorous, 11-year-old Lewis is ashamed of being the brunt of bullies without the spunk or strength to defend himself, his Uncle Jonathan, the practicing wizard, shows him the contents of his great-grandfather's Civil War chest and tells the story of how that peaceable ancestor avoided combat. Lewis asks to keep the old coin he wore as a good-luck piece and soon discovers that it is a magic amulet capable of conjuring up new strength, courage, and sudden respect. But it also summons forth a frightening figure in dark robes that lunges at him unexpectedly, and his best friend Rose Rita takes the amulet and hides it for his own protection. He ferrets it out by stealth, and only quick thinking and fast action on the part of Mrs. Zimmerman, the witch next door, Uncle Jonathan, and Rose Rita save him from being possessed by the shadowy haunt from the past.

154. Bragdon, Elspeth. <u>That Jud!</u> New York: Viking Press, 1957. Illus. by Georges Schreiber. Grades 4-6.

Some say it crossly, some admiringly, some lovingly. "That Jud" is a trial to everyone in the Maine fishing village except Captain Ben whom the town appointed his guardian after his parents' death. Jud, 12, can be rebellious and heedless from time to time but never deliberately mean or dishonest. He did break Homer's boathouse windows in a fit of pique, but he helped replace them. His greatest source of satisfaction is the cabin of his own he is building on a tiny island, and his greatest desire is to find a small stove for it. The opportunity arises to earn money for one when a wealthy summer resident, Mr. York, hires him to care for his outboard motorboat. Suspicion is pointed at Jud when a mysterious fire erupts in Mr. York's shed which Jud just happens to be on hand to extinguish, but many voices rise to his defense, the true culprit confesses, and Jud is exonerated and touted as the hero he is.

155. Bulla, Clyde Robert. <u>White Bird</u>. New York: Thomas Y. Crowell, 1966. Illus. by Leonard Weisgard. Grades 3-5.

John Thomas is rescued and reared in the Tennessee

wilderness by reclusive, taciturn misanthrope Luke Vail after his cradle is carried Moses-like down the flooding river in which his pioneer parents perished. Denied a pet because he might become emotionally attached to it, John adopts a wounded albino crow and nurses it to health, only to have it stolen by scoundrels. Restrained from following them by Luke, John runs away and eventually finds his bird dead. He returns voluntarily to Luke, bringing with him a subliminal lesson in love and trust.

156. Burch, Robert. Skinny. New York: Viking Press, 1964. Illus. by Don Sibley. Grades 4-6.

Skinny is the descriptive sobriquet of the naive but engaging Georgia orphan boy who has reached the age of 11 without setting foot inside a school or learning to read and write, because his shiftless father, an alcoholic sharecropper, saw no value in it. When his Pa dies he is offered a home by benevolent Miss Bessie who operates the local rustic hostelry. She wants to adopt him officially, but the town fathers look askance upon a single woman's assuming that responsibility. For awhile it appears that their dreams will materialize when Daddy Rabbit takes up residence at the hotel and takes a shine to Miss Bessie and Skinny, but hopes go aglimmering when the lure of the road again beckons him. Skinny accepts his fate with a certain aplomb, makes friends his own age at the orphanage, learns to read and write, and looks forward to holidays and summer vacation with Miss Bessie and the rest of the hotel "family."

157. Burnett, Frances Hodgson. The Secret Garden. Philadelphia: J. B. Lippincott, 1962 (c1911). Illus. by Tasha Tudor. Grades 5-8.

Three tragic, unloved and unloving, parallel lives gradually change direction, eventually to meld in joy and affection when orphaned Mary is sent to her uncle's estate in England upon her parents' death in India and discovers the magical secret garden that becomes the catalyst in dispelling her uncle's bitterness, her cousin Colin's fears, and her own rancor. Industry, exercise, fresh air and determination are nature's panacea for both physical and emotional maladies.

158. Byars, Betsy. After the Goat Man. New York: Viking Press, 1974. Illus. by Ronald Himler. Grades 4-6.

Three single-parent situations occur in this story:

Figgy lives with his grandfather, Ada with her father, and Harold with his mother. Harold is a self-indulgent, egocentric, obese boy who takes lugubrious pleasure in wallowing in his own misery. His only friend is Ada who is totally unselfconscious, tolerant, thoughtful and sympathetic. Then diffident, defensive Figgy moves in, and Harold, with Ada's guidance, learns to become sensitive to the misfortunes of others. Figgy's grandfather is the taciturn "Goat Man," an eccentric recluse whose cabin has been condemned to make way for a superhighway. The broken old man cannot adjust to city life in the row of concrete block houses where he has been relocated, and he returns to the cabin to defy the bulldozers. Figgy's injury in a bike mishap en route to his grandfather's defense with his new friends forces his grandfather to abandon his campaign but not his dignity. Ada's father promises to find them a more suitable home.

159. Clark, Ann Nolan. Secret of the Andes. New York: Viking Press, 1952. Illus. by Jean Charlot. Grades 5-7.

Cusi has lived for eight years, as long as he can remember, high in the Andes in the solitude of secret Hidden Valley with Chuto, his mentor, herding the sacred flock of Inca llamas. From an overhanging rock he can look down and see a family with three children like ants far below, and he yearns to be part of a family. Two unexpected visitors to their mountain sanctuary change his pastoral life and give him the opportunity he seeks. He wears the golden earplugs of Inca royalty and is being groomed to be keeper of the ancient treasure and traditions. The time has come for him to make his pilgrimage to Cuzco, bringing the symbolic gift of llamas. His dream comes true when he is asked to join a large, rollicking Indian family on holiday in the city, but he is quickly disillusioned with their Spanish corruptions and habit of sleeping indoors. He recognizes that his place is with Chuto, father of his choice, as guardian of the gold and llamas. He returns home, takes the vows, is shown the secret cave, and is told the story of his blood parents.

160. Cleaver, Vera, and Bill Cleaver. Where the Lilies Bloom. Philadelphia: J. B. Lippincott, 1969. Illus. by Jim Spanfeller. Grades 5-7.

Under the shadows of the Great Smoky Mountains

Roy Luther lies dying, and 14-year-old Mary Call has promised him that she will keep the family intact, not accept charity, and never permit childlike Devola, 18, to marry importuning Kiser Pease, the instrument of their oppression and poverty. With proud fortitude and grim determination she takes the helm, buries her father clandestinely up on the mountain as he desired, exploits Kiser Pease with Machiavellian cunning, and launches a family enterprise of wildcrafting, the gathering of medicinal roots and herbs for sale. Her brave but shaky ship of state founders during the demoniacally inclement winter when Pease's sister arrives and threatens to evict them from their crumbling cabin. In the end she cannot prevent the suddenly mature Devola from marrying the mellowed and repentant Pease, whose love for Devola proves to be salvation also for Mary Call, Romey, 10, and Ima Dean, 5.

161. Cunningham, Julia. <u>Dorp Dead.</u> New York: Pantheon, 1965. Illus. by James Spanfeller. Grades 4-7.

Since his grandmother's death, 11-year-old Gilly has been a cipher in an orphan asylum where to gain privacy and a semblance of dignity he feigns stupidity and ineptitude, although he is actually a brilliant boy. His few leisure hours are stolen in a deserted, decaying ancient tower where he meets another loner, "The Hunter," one day when he runs away in defiance. As punishment for his recalcitrance he is bound out to a laddermaker feared for his taciturnity and pathological punctuality. At first he enjoys the comfort, order, peace and quiet of his new establishment, until he discovers the sinister plot of the diabolical man to dehumanize and enslave him as he has his dog. Utilizing his sharp wit, Gilly makes his harrowing escape from the fortified house, only to be cornered in the tower by the fiendish Mr. Kobalt, bent on his destruction. He is saved by the dog he defended, and boy and dog seek out "The Hunter" who has promised them a home. Only later does Gilly learn to spell.

162. Fleischman, Sid. <u>Chancy and the Grand Rascal.</u> Boston: Little, Brown, 1966. Illus. by Eric von Schmidt. Grades 5-8.

Chancy lost both parents during the Civil War, and he and his younger sisters and brother were parceled out to whoever would make a home for them. Now that he's grown, Chancy sallies forth to reunite the family, trundling his worldly possessions in a wheelbarrow, intending to board a steamer for Paducah to collect his sister Indiana first. Two days later he is duped out of all his money by a villainous old jackanapes and left with a suitcase of eggs hatching like popcorn. He and the chicks make camp on an island in the Ohio River where he joins forces with his uncle, an audacious adventurer, roguish raconteur, and jack of all trades, and together they pursue their quest, flummoxing their adversaries and regaling their confederates with wits, whoppers, and derring-do. They deliver Indiana, 11, from the penurious scoundrel who has held her in servitude and trace Jamie, 9, and Mirandy, 7, to Kansas just in time to save the town histrionically from jayhawkers disguised as Indians. A grateful citizenry offers Uncle Will the mayoralty, it is accepted as a challenge, and the reunited family decides to stop rambling.

163. Flory, Jane. Faraway Dream. Boston: Houghton Mifflin, 1968. Illus. by the author. Grades 5-7.

Timid, compassionate Miss Charlotte chooses spunky redhead Maggy, 12, among all the orphans at the Seafarers Safe Harbor orphanage to become her apprentice in the millinery enterprise she conducts from the front parlor of her sister and brother-in-law's home in post-Revolutionary Philadelphia. The Whitsons and their daughter, churlish social climbers, try and nearly succeed in making groveling servants of Maggy and Miss Charlotte, but Maggy, trained in survival techniques on the waterfront, proves less tractable than her mentor, and her spirit inculcates in Miss Charlotte the will to stand her ground. Maggy's solace when injustice and oppression rankle is her dream that her shipwrecked father will appear one day and carry them off in style to the consternation and envy of the Whitsons. It happens just that way, except that their liberator is not Maggy's father (who died valiantly when his ship foundered) but Miss Charlotte's suitor, a French gentleman of tasteful means, who makes a loving home for Maggy as well.

164. Gage, Wilson. Big Blue Island. Cleveland: World Publishing, 1964. Illus. by Glen Rounds. Grades 5-6.

After his father's desertion and his mother's death from tuberculosis, 11-year-old Darrell is sent from Detroit to live with his only known relative, a great-uncle who lives alone on a river island in Tennessee with no plumbing or electricity. Darrell is resentful of the lack of amenities, the imposed solitude, and especially the old codger's acerbity, and he plans to run away to Florida where living is easy, but he lacks both money and opportunity, being a virtual prisoner on the island because the old man padlocks his rowboat. When his uncle bets him a dollar he can't catch one of the great blue herons that winter there, he sees his chance to earn pocket money and sets about the task with determination until he learns that it is impossible, illegal, and dangerous to trap the creatures when his uncle stumbles on the snares and hurts his back. The ranger convinces the boy that it is actually desirable to live on the island like a sort of permanent camping trip and persuades the curmudgeon to buy the boy an old motorboat so he will have some mobility.

165. Lampman, Evelyn Sibley. Navaho Sister. Garden City, N.Y.: Doubleday, 1956. Illus. by Paul Lantz. Grades 5-7.

Sad Girl, 12, and her grandmother, She-Who-Knows-Much-Trouble, are pitied on their reservation because they have no surviving family. Sad Girl is reluctant to leave her grandmother and go to boarding school to be Americanized, but Grandmother insists, and Sad Girl is launched upon the most exciting and terrifying adventure of her life. Her first momentous decision is to choose a name, Rose Smith, the surname of which Grandmother will share. Making new friends from other reservations and adjusting to strange customs, language, food, and modern technology are all major hurdles to surmount, but there are compensations too, such as her first state fair, movie, and Christmas, not to mention earning the first money of her own. Her biggest concern is her lack of a family and how it will affect her status at school if it becomes known. Just as she is belatedly assured that it makes no difference, her long-lost uncle appears who also happens to be the father of her best friend and roommate.

166. _____. The Shy Stegosaurus of Indian Springs. Garden City, N.Y.: Doubleday, 1962. Illus. by Paul Galdone. Grades 5-7.

When Huck returns home from Indian boarding school to his grandfather's hut on the reservation for the summer, he is startled to discover George the Stegosaurus inhabiting the hot mineral springs where he does the laundry, but he is delighted to make friends with Joey and Joan [see 60] who are spending the summer with their aunt following their mother's marriage to an archaeology professor. Huck has no friends among his own kind because they ridicule his grandfather Opalo, a truculent old medicine man who speaks only the Klickitat tongue. The new chief enjoins Opalo to board in town with one of the progressive families the following winter, while Opalo just as obdurately refuses to relinquish his traditional life on the desert. Brainless but instinctive George inadvertently provides Opalo a spectacular opportunity for restoring his tarnished prestige at the annual harvest festival by his persistence in watching the Indian-wrestling and his insatiable appetite for overripe bananas. A compromise is achieved for Huck's grandfather.

167. Lawrence, Mildred. Peachtree Island. New York: Harcourt, Brace, 1948. Illus. by Mary Stevens. Grades 4-6.

Cissie, 9, is sent to Peachtree Island off the shore of Lake Erie to stay with Uncle Eben, whom she has never met, while the aunt with whom she lives is away. Uncle Eben turns out to be a true kindred spirit, and Mrs. Halloran, his housekeeper, is a grandmotherly dumpling, but Jody, the boy next door, taunts her that boys are better than girls when she tries to be useful around Uncle Eben's peach orchard in the hopes that he will let her stay permanently. Besides assisting Uncle Eben, Cissie helps Mrs. Halloran make apple butter, goes ice fishing for Christmas money with her uncle, crosses an ice bridge to a neighboring island to make friends with rich but lonely Araminta, and goes for a sleigh ride with her friend Melinda. When trouble strikes at Araminta's island, she comes to stay with Cissie and pitches right in with the farm chores. At year's end when the harvest is in, Uncle Eben acknowledges Cissie's responsibility and indispensability, and even Jody concedes that girls are almost as good as boys.

168. Lexau, Joan M. Benjie. New York: Dial Press, 1964. Illus. by Don Bolognese. Grades K-2.

Benjie is the most bashful boy his Granny has ever seen and she despairs of him since he is to start school in a few weeks. He hates to talk to anyone, and always peeks out to see if the coast is clear before venturing outside the door alone. He is especially intimidated by the formidable bakery lady. One day after church Gran-

Bibliography

ny loses one of her keepsake earrings. While she is napping he goes out to search for it again. He is about to give up when he remembers that nobody looked in the bakery where they stopped after church and he slips in the back room while the bakery lady is engaged. When she discovers him he is compelled to explain his mission to prevent her from calling the police. Then she even helps him sift through the trash and the earring is found. Granny is overjoyed to get it back but notes with a twinkle that something else is missing: one bashful, tongue-tied boy.

169. _____. Benjie on His Own. New York: Dial Press, 1970. Illus. by Don Bolognese. Grades K-2.

When Benjie's grandmother is not there to meet him after school as usual [see 168], he is concerned about her but not sure he can find his way home alone through the ghetto streets. He is chased by a dog and accosted by teenage toughs but finally arrives to find her desperately ill. Resourcefully he calls for an ambulance from the police emergency box. He doesn't want to leave her alone while he waits to guide the ambulance team but has no one to turn to. Finally in desperation he yells, "HELP! Please somebody HELP!" At last the impassive neighborhood rallies round, and helping hands reassure Granny that he will be well cared for while she is in the hospital.

170. Lindgren, Astrid. Rasmus and the Vagabond. New York: Viking Press, 1960. Illus. by Eric Palmquist. Grades 4-6.

Only curly-headed girls are ever adopted from Vaesterhaga orphanage, and 9-year-old Rasmus' hair is hopelessly straight. Miss Hawk, moreover, is frightfully rigid, and when he earns her enmity he knows he must flee, though he is reluctant to part with his best friend Gunnar. Setting off in search of parents, he falls in instead with an amiable and honorable tramp named Oscar. Together they cadge meals, are mistaken for thieves, get pursued by both the real gangsters and the sheriff, but are eventually vindicated and see justice served. When sympathetic foster parents finally materialize, he turns down their offer in order to remain with Oscar but recommends his friend Gunnar for the post. Down the road apiece Oscar surprises him with a real home and even a mother who has straight hair like his own.

171. Means, Florence Crannell. <u>Shuttered Windows</u>. Boston: Houghton Mifflin, 1938. Illus. by Armstrong Sperry. Grades 7-9.

Orphaned Harriet, 16, is offered a home with kindly Reverend Trindle and his wife where she can pursue her music career, but she has a strong compulsion to find her only living relative, the great-grandmother she has never seen. An honor student from a middle-class Minneapolis milieu, she is appalled and ashamed by the poverty, segregation, illiteracy and superstition of Granny and her neighbors in rural, insular South Carolina and wants to return with the Trindles. But she is also entranced by her stately Granny, the loud and easy laughter shared by her race, the spirit of unity in the little church, and a handsome boy with musical talent of his own with a desire to help his people at a grass-roots level. She decides to stay for one semester. At boarding school nearby she remains aloof from the local girls and makes friends with another cosmopolite. The two are accepted into school life only as they become more tolerant and find they have something to contribute. At semester's end she elects to remain and cast her lot with Granny and Richard in the place of her ancestry.

172. O'Dell, Scott. <u>Zia</u>. Boston: Houghton Mifflin, 1976. Grades 5-6.

Cupeno Indian girl Zia's sole surviving relative besides her younger brother Mando is her mother's sister Karana, who has been subsisting on the bleak, uninhabited Island of the Blue Dolphins with no companionship but that of a wild dog. Zia's obsessive desire to find her aunt impels her to follow the padres from her distant village, attempt a hazardous but abortive sea voyage, and remain behind when Mando and the Chumash Indians escape from the tyranny of the mission at Santa Barbara. For her abetment of the escape she is imprisoned and tortured at the nearby garrison. A sympathetic padre effects the rescue of both aunt and niece, and they are finally united. Too soon the cruel realities of colonial Spanish civilization take their toll of Karana, who dies, but not before imparting wordlessly a sense of independence and personal dignity to the 14-year-old girl, who returns to her mother's people with Karana's big dog at her side.

173. Pope, Elizabeth Marie. <u>The Sherwood Ring</u>. Boston: Houghton Mifflin, 1958. Illus. by Evaline Ness. Grades 6-9.

On her father's death, 17-year-old Peggy Grahame goes to live with her irascible elderly uncle on the family's ancestral estate, Rest-and-be-thankful, in upstate New York where she encounters Pat Thorne, a young British historian skulking about the property researching Revolutionary history. Her uncle is peremptorily loath to share old family secrets, but the lively ghosts who seem to step right out of their somber portraits are not, and appear frequently to unfold to Peggy a fascinating tale of wartime romance and intrigue that draws a prophetic parallel to Peggy's budding, clandestine romance with Pat. Uncle Enos' sudden illness stimulates the search for the missing chapter of the story that brings history full circle, links the Grahame and Thorne families, and closes the schism.

174. Shotwell, Louisa R. Magdalena. New York: Viking Press, 1971. Illus. by Lilian Obligado. Grades 5-6.
When shy Magdalena, 11, is transferred to the Intellectually Gifted sixth-grade classroom, some of her classmates deride the long, thick braids her old-fashioned Puerto Rican grandmother makes her wear, and when her friend, odd old Miss Lillie, provides the opportunity she wastes no time in having her hair cropped, causing her horrified grandmother to think she has been bewitched by American frippery. In the meantime, another Puerto Rican girl, the victim of a wretched homelife and an atrocious behavior problem whom everyone calls Spook, is transferred into her class, and the principal asks Magdalena to befriend her, a seemingly insurmountable assignment. The girls' mutual respect for Miss Lillie and Magdalena's grandmother, Nani, eventually draws them together and modifies Spook's behavior, but Nani remains intractably suspicious of Miss Lillie and her Americanizing influence. Miss Lillie's collapse from malnutrition reconciles the two women, and Magdalena and Spook write the two best stories for the class literary magazine.

175. Spyri, Johanna. Heidi. Philadelphia: David McKay, 1923 (c1880). Illus. by Anne Alexander. Grades 5-6.
Here is the beloved classic in which 5-year-old Heidi comes to live with her grandfather, the truculent Alm-Uncle, endears herself to him and to Peter the goatherd and his grandmother, only to be carried off again to the city to be companion to the wealthy invalid Clara. Her homesickness is physically and mentally debilitating in spite of her love for Clara, and the dis-

cerning doctor prescribes a return to her natural habitat. There she repatriates her grandfather into human society and brings light into Peter's grandmother's darkness. When Clara pays a visit to the Alm, Peter's jealousy precipitates a crisis, but he atones by assisting Heidi and her grandfather in restoring the stricken girl to health. Clara's grateful father bestows beneficences on all.

176. Streatfeild, Noel. <u>The Children on the Top Floor.</u> New York: Random House, 1964. Illus. by Jillian Willett. Grades 5-8.

Suave bachelor TV personality Malcolm Master acquires an instant family following an emotional Christmas Eve performance: four infants whose mothers left them on his doorstep as gifts. In reality, small children terrify the great star, so the four babes are spirited off to the top floor of his London house to grow up in sheltered solitude where he seldom sees them, their needs ministered to by old-fashioned Nannie, "Mistermaster's" secretary Aunt Mamie, the cook, and the chauffeur. They attain immediate notoriety as the Master Quads, which Mamie cannily capitalizes on by hiring an agent and signing the children for TV endorsements. The advertisers keep the kids supplied with their products, and they only venture from the house to be driven to and from the TV studios until the arrival of Mrs. Comfort, the new governess, who begins normalizing their cloistered existence. Meanwhile, Mr. Master is shipwrecked in the South Seas and feared dead, and Thomas, eldest of the four 10-year-olds, injures his back, terminating the Quads' commercial career. It appears that they will have to go to an orphans' home until Mr. Master suddenly reappears to be a real father to them.

177. Talbot, Charlene Joy. <u>A Home with Aunt Florry.</u> New York: Atheneum, 1974. Grades 5-7.

Accustomed to the accoutrements of wealth and ease, 12-year-old twins Jason and Wendy, orphaned by their parents' plane crash, are appalled when they come to live in New York with their bohemian, iconoclastic Aunt Florry in a derelict newspaper plant. Moreover, she is an inveterate junk collector who never cleans house and keeps common pigeons in the loft. Robbed of the security of order and regulation in their lives, they are first frightened and then resentful at having to help with chores which consist of opening cans or heating TV dinners for meals, hanging the laundry to dry on the roof, feeding and exercising the pigeons, and scavenging in trash bins for wood to stoke the pot-bellied stove. When Aunt Florry is hospitalized for a fractured hip, the two must practice self-reliance, and they begin to appreciate their independent and unorthodox lifestyle. But the day of their eviction to make way for urban renewal quickly approaches. Resourceful Aunt Florry, however, has already planned a replacement home which satisfies both the children's bourgeois attorney and her own idiosyncrasies.

178. Van Stockum, Hilda. <u>Andries</u>. New York: Viking Press, 1942. Illus. by the author. Grades 5-6.

Upon his parents' accidental death, 10-year-old Andries is received reluctantly by his misanthropic bachelor uncle and his lazy, selfish housekeeper, who live in a large house in the Dutch countryside. He is not permitted to slide down the bannister or climb trees, activities which are regarded as willful misdemeanors in the drab household. In school the city boy is taunted and teased by his classmates, and he lashes back in self-defense, earning the reputation of reprobate. Only the rambunctious children in the little house nearby befriend the unhappy lad and give him a chance to show his gentle nature. Planning to run away one night, he gives the housekeeper a bad fright and she terminates her service. The understanding mother from the little house arranges a sympathetic replacement who charms the boy and tames the curmudgeon. The two marry, and Andries acquires a second set of doting parents.

179. Wier, Ester. <u>The Barrel</u>. New York: David McKay, 1966. Illus. by Carl Kidwell. Grades 5-7.

For seven years Chance has been shunted from one foster home to another after his father abandoned him to the Child Welfare Agency up North. Now at 12, he is being sent to family he didn't know existed in the Florida Everglades, his maternal grandmother and his 15-year-old brother Turpem. Their father was a braggart who instilled in his older son the idea that courage and daring are all that count, and he swaggers and boasts before Chance, who inherited his dead mother's gentle disposition and slight build and who, as a city boy, nurtures a healthy respect for the alligators, wild boars, and poisonous snakes that infest the swamp. Chance soon realizes that Turpem's bravery is nothing but bravado, and later proves that he and his doughty runt pup are no cowards when a hurricane blocks their normal egress to civilization and they must detour through dreaded Doomsday Slough, Turpem's nemesis. Resentment is forgotten as the boys finally become friends, to the delight of their wise but simple Granny.

180. _____. The Loner. New York: David McKay, 1963. Illus. by Christine Price. Grades 5-7.

The boy has known no life but that of itinerant crop picker, has had no friend but the golden-haired girl whose family he has been traveling with. When she is killed, the grieving boy strikes out blindly on his own and is found starving and exhausted in sheep-grazing terrain in the Montana foothills by Boss, the Amazonian owner of the ranch who has brought her flock to winter pasture herself in order to track down the grizzly that killed her beloved grown son Ben. The boy selects the name David at random from Boss' Bible, and she sets about teaching him the intricacies and rigors of herding sheep, subconsciously comparing him to her flawless Ben. The laconic woman and the willful loner misunderstand one another's motives, but David quietly learns. When Ben's widow Angie tells him to use his own good judgment, he summons the confidence to save Tex from the bear trap and kill the behemoth, his personal Goliath, to win his own place in the family and his first home.

PROTRACTED ABSENCE OF PARENT(S)

181. Anckarsvard, Karin. <u>Aunt Vinnie's Invasion.</u> New York: Harcourt, Brace and World, 1962. Illus. by William M. Hutchinson. Grades 5-6.
    The six Hallsenius children are sent to stay with their independent, sensible, unsentimental, elderly Aunt Lavinia in a Stockholm suburb while their parents, professional photographers, are on assignment in Africa. Aunt Vinnie will not tolerate dogs, but 12-year-old Lollie is determined to bring her mutt Piazzo along and ingeniously smuggles him in and out of her room until Aunt Vinnie catches on and lets her keep him. She further captivates the youngsters when 9-year-old Per wanders away from school in a reverie and she squares his truancy with school authorities with a white lie. The greatest test of her patience and wisdom comes when belligerent Sam, 13, accidentally stuns his brother Anders, 16, in an altercation, believes he has killed him, and runs away from the scene of the crime. Later he redeems himself by heroically forestalling a deliberately set explosion. The children demonstrate their appreciation and affection for Aunt Vinnie on her birthday.

182. ─────────. <u>Aunt Vinnie's Victorious Six.</u> New York: Harcourt, Brace and World, 1964. Illus. by William M. Hutchinson. Grades 5-6.
    Anders and Annika, 15, are absorbed with members of the opposite sex as spring comes to Nordvik, and Lottie is mortified when she accidentally breaks Aunt Vinnie's best antique crystal bowl and goes to great lengths, almost getting arrested, to replace it. But it is Per who causes the greatest stir in his beloved aunt's life, instructing her how to enter the soccer pool, entreating her to help him with his homework at the crack of dawn in the bushes behind the school, and causing great concern when the shy little African boy he has made friends with despite the language barrier disappears and is feared drowned. The boy is found unexpectedly, but even more surprisingly, Aunt Vinnie wins the soccer pool and abides by the Hallsenius' family motto, "One for all and all for one."

183. Angelo, Valenti. <u>The Bells of Bleecker Street.</u> New York: Viking Press, 1949. Illus. by the author. Grades 5-8.

    Italian and Irish mingle amicably on Bleecker Street in Greenwich Village, their lives regulated by the carillons of the two big churches, Our Lady of Pompeii and St. Patrick's, intoning time till World War II is over and their loved ones return. Joey Enrico's father has been fighting in Italy near his ancestral home and has not seen his family for two years. Joey, 12, and his friends occupy themselves with baseball games, music lessons, and innocent mischief. Finally the chimes peal victory and the end of the war, and Joey's father returns to get reacquainted with his little family and the baby daughter he has never seen. The story closes with their glorious Christmas celebration within the circle of relatives and friends, always dominated by the bells, an ode to the urban family life of mixed cultures when circumstances were less volatile.

184. _____. <u>Nino.</u> New York: Viking Press, 1938. Illus. by the author. Grades 5-8.

    This is the heartwarming story of the first eight years in the life of Nino, an Italian peasant boy living with his mother in his grandfather's comfortable cottage, awaiting money from his father who is in America working to make passage for them to join him. It is also the saga of the ebb and flow of Italian village life as it has throbbed for centuries, ordained by the seasons, the crops, the religious traditions, and the folk customs. And finally, it is the tenderly told tale of primordial friendship and sacrosanct loyalty. Nino is a clever and imaginative boy whose ambition is to become an artist in emulation of the village woodcarver. He is reared with wisdom and compassion in an atmosphere rich in intangible values if lacking in materialistic appurtenances. Their eventual bittersweet departure is tempered by the fond memories they are free to take and the looming expectations that fill their horizon.

185. Armstrong, William H. <u>Sounder.</u> New York: Harper and Row, 1969. Illus. by James Barkley. Grades 4-6.

    The deep-baying mastiff adopted the man when he was just a pup, and the two are inseparable. Now the man has six mouths to feed, but the coons and possums have gone to earth with the coming of chill winter winds. One morning the oldest boy wakens to the smell of cooking pork for only the second time in his life. Before the day is out the sheriff has come to arrest his father for stealing a ham and some sausage links. As deputies take him away in shackles, Sounder bursts from the boy's grasp, tries to follow, and is shot down in the road. With half his head and shoulder missing, he drags himself into the woods to die. The boy visits his father in jail and experiences the law's disregard for human dignity. The father is sentenced to hard labor and taken away. One day Sounder reappears, hideously scarred, missing an eye, ear and leg, and also mute. The boy tries vainly to find his father but meets instead the opportunity for education. Years later the father returns, crippled, and Sounder gives voice once more. The two old veterans soon go to their final reward, but Sounder has kept the faith.

186. Bawden, Nina. The House of Secrets. Philadelphia: J. B. Lippincott, 1963. Illus. by Wendy Worth. Grades 5-8.

Following their mother's illness and death and their father's ensuing nervous breakdown, the three Mallory children are sent from their hospitable farm home in Africa to their aunt's boarding house in cold, cramped England. Unaccustomed to children, Aunt Mabel seems as chilly as the wintry seaside climate, but the children, John, 12, Mary, 11, and Ben, 7, quickly make friends with her eccentric, non-paying boarders. Seeking diversion, they find a secret subterranean passage to the deserted mansion next door which disgorges priceless treasures and a disagreeable piano-playing orphan girl who may be Aunt Mabel's long-lost baby girl. An unwitting brush with the law produces unexpected results, an end to their poverty, a home for the orphan, an affectionate response from Aunt Mabel, but best of all, the news that Dad is returning to them weak but well.

187. Benary-Isbert, Margot. The Ark. New York: Harcourt, Brace and World, 1953. Translated by Clara and Richard Winston. Grades 5-8.

Two frigid attic rooms with a dour landlady look palatial to the four Lechow children and their mother, homeless refugees in post-war Germany, optimistic for the safe return of their father who has been in a Russian prison camp. Mother's ingenuity, generosity of spirit, and sewing skill help fend the wolf from the door, and the younger children, 7 and 9, make friends and attend school. An attraction for animals and an auspicious Christmas-caroling pilgrimage into the countryside win jobs for the older children, 14 and 15, at Rowan Farm where they set up housekeeping in an old railway car they dub the "Ark." It is there that the entire family is eventually reunited. Shy 14-year-old Margret makes friends in turn with the petulant landlady, whom she captivates and converts, and with Marri, the reclusive "bee witch," from whom she learns the secret not of how to forget sorrows in the aftermath of war, but of how to "remember differently."

188. Bradley, Duane. Meeting with a Stranger. Philadelphia: J. B. Lippincott, 1964. Illus. by E. Harper Johnson. Grades 4-6.

Left in charge of his father's flock while he goes to Addis Ababa to submit to eye surgery, young Teffera is wary of trusting the disarming American who wants to experiment with the weak, sickly sheep because of the experience of his Ethiopian forebears in misplacing their trust in foreigners. When his progressive uncle persuades his influential grandfather to support Mr. Jones' program, Teffera hides the best of the flock, fearing that the American with the alien mien will kill them to gain control over the village. Mr. Jones calmly agrees to use the isolated half as a control group. Still unconvinced, Teffera devises a secret plan to test Mr. Jones' sincerity, but feels remorseful when the gentle, patient American passes with flying colors, because he has befriended the boys of the village and begun a school for them. Teffera and his friend, who has been even more stubborn and suspicious, atone for their doubts.

189. Burch, Robert. Queenie Peavy. New York: Viking Press, 1966. Illus. by Jerry Lazare. Grades 4-6.

Rebellious Queenie, 13, defensive of her incarcerated father, vents her aggressions in destructive rock throwing and causes her chief tormentor to break his leg. No one believes her when she is unjustly accused of breaking windows in the church and she is on the brink of being sent to the reformatory. Given a chance to redeem herself when a classmate collapses from malnutrition, Queenie decides to turn over a new leaf. Her father comes home on parole and reveals his true character, and Queenie learns to handle her disillusionment and rely on her own aptitudes. Exculpated of the charges against her, she gains the acceptance of her junior high classmates in their rural Georgia town during the Great Depression.

190. Carlson, Natalie Savage. <u>Ann Aurelia and Dorothy.</u> New York: Harper and Row, 1968. Illus. by Dale Payson. Grades 4-5.

Her mother's new husband doesn't like her, so Ann Aurelia has been assigned to a succession of foster homes. Her new foster mother, Mrs. Hicken, is as comfortable as an old shoe and seems genuinely fond of her, even getting involved in PTA, so she feels no need for her real mother any longer. She has found her first bosom buddy in Dorothy, a black girl in her fifth-grade class, and she likes her new school. She and Dorothy have fun concocting weird snacks, shopping in the supermarket, being in the Safety Patrol together, saving Miss Wyckoff from drowning on a field trip, making a spooky Halloween mask, and staging a surprise party for Miss Bennett. When her real mother turns up unexpectedly, having divorced Mr. Lacey and avowing her mistake, Ann Aurelia initially refuses to forgive and return to her until Dorothy helps her to empathize with her mother's loneliness. Mrs. Hicken finds them an apartment near school, and Ann and Dorothy go to visit Mrs. Hicken and her new foster child.

191. Coblentz, Catherine Cate. <u>Martin and Abraham Lincoln.</u> Chicago: Children's Press, 1947. Illus. by Trientja. Grades 2-3.

Young Martin's father is in Andersonville prison during the Civil War and his mother is sorely pressed to feed Martin and his three little sisters. A kindly neighboring farmer gives them fresh vegetables in return for Martin's help in selling his produce door-to-door in Washington, D. C., but they never have staples like flour, sugar, butter or eggs. On one journey to the city, the farmer leaves Martin to rest in the park across from the Capitol. Sitting deep in reverie on the Capitol steps, he is startled by the tall shadow of President Lincoln who pauses to console the forlorn little boy and confirm his pride in his father.

192. Collier, James Lincoln. <u>Give Dad My Best.</u> New York: Four Winds, 1976. Grades 6-8.

The fortunes of the Lundquist family have been declining steadily since the onset of the Great Depression when their musician father lost his steady employment but refused to soil his hands with menial labor. Their mother lost her mind from anxiety and had to be institutionalized, and now there is no money to feed or clothe the three children, rent and utilities are months in arrears, yet Dad spends what he makes playing occasional "gigs" on expensive records, beer and cigarettes for himself, exhorting them to "look on the bright side." Fearing bankruptcy and breakup of the family, and juggling boyish dreams of becoming a baseball star with adult schemes to make money, 14-year-old Jack takes part-time jobs and frequently contemplates larceny. Facing eviction, he finally summons the nerve to steal the ill-gotten gains of his employer but salves his conscience by making partial restitution when he realizes dissolution of the family is inevitable because his Dad's personality will never change.

193. Corcoran, Barbara. <u>The Winds of Time</u>. New York: Atheneum, 1974. Illus. by Gail Owens. Grades 6-9.

Teenage Gail becomes the ward of her disarmingly solicitous but malicious uncle when her mother returns to the mental hospital, and she seeks the first opportunity for escape. It comes when Uncle Chad's car crashes on a snowy mountain road in Colorado and he is pinned in the wreckage. Gail, unharmed, follows her cat Sylvester down an overgrown lane straight into a fairyland of the forgotten splendor of the nineteenth century, the munificent wooded estate of the pioneering, financiering Partridge dynasty. Elderly Mrs. Partridge and her bachelor son, now recluses, graciously take her in without question, yet Mrs. Partridge's grandson Christopher, a serious naturalist, is suspicious of her until he becomes convinced her story is true. While awaiting word from Gail's honorable but capricious father, whose last known address was Hawaii, Mrs. Partridge predicts the teenager's checkered future in Tarot cards, and they all connive to keep her out of the clutches of the underhanded, overbearing sheriff and wily Uncle Chad. When her affable father finally appears, the Partridges offer him a job and a place in the family for the summer.

194. Farjeon, Annabel. <u>Maria Lupin</u>. New York: Abelard-Schuman, 1967. Illus. by James Hunt. Grades 5-6.

Because of a forged Scarlatti sonata, 10-year-old Maria meets a renowned but enigmatic old pianist and becomes his pupil, beginning a secret life she must conceal from her mother who is in a constant state of anxiety and agitation since her husband's disappearance three years earlier. Maria longs to know the details but her mother won't discuss it, and the lonely and preoccupied girl finds it difficult to concentrate on schoolwork or make friends among her classmates. Her latent musical ability gives her purpose and direction, but to make friends out of former foes she is compelled to knock one boy senseless. When she suddenly spills her secret to her mother on Guy Fawkes Day in London, Mrs. Lupin in turn unburdens herself to the aging musician, and when he is stricken ill she is able to nurse him back to health. At his recovery celebration he announces that he has been making worldwide inquiries about the missing Mr. Lupin who will soon rejoin them.

195. Kleberger, Ilse. Traveling with Oma. New York: Atheneum, 1970. Illus. by Hans Behrens. Translated by Belinda McGill. Grades 4-6.

Dauntless, roller-skating Grandmother Oma subdues an inept burglar, rehabilitates him, then borrows his conveyance, a bright green gypsy caravan drawn by a peculiar horse named Max, for a glorious, hilarious summer of adventure and misadventure with her three young charges, Jan, Peter, and Bridget. Along the way, with Oma's guidance, daydreamer Peter learns to separate fact from fancy, and adolescent Jan learns that smoking does not necessarily make the man. The quartet plus Max finally succeed in reuniting burglar/magician Mario with his circus family.

196. L'Engle, Madeleine. A Wrinkle in Time. New York: Farrar, Straus and Giroux, 1962. Grades 5-8.

With the help of three unearthly beings, Mrs. Whatsit, Mrs. Which, and Mrs. Who, the two most sensitive of the four Murry children, Meg, 14, and Charles Wallace, 5, along with Calvin, a high school friend of Meg's, travel a tesseract, or wrinkle in time, to new planets beyond their galaxy existing in a fifth dimension. They go in search of their father, a physicist who disappeared abruptly while on a secret and perilous government mission. There they consult the Happy Medium and are directed to the planet of Camazotz, ruled by the Dark Thing. The magical trio cannot remain with them there because their powers are insufficient. The children find themselves in a menacing world of regimentation and mechanization. A disembodied brain called IT mesmerically tries to control their minds. Charles Wallace succumbs but Meg and Calvin resist long enough to rescue her father from the transparent column in which he is imprisoned and "tesser" to a safe planet. Meg alone must return to Camazotz to wrest Charles Wallace's mind from the clutches of IT with love as her sole weapon.

197. Ransome, Arthur. <u>Swallows and Amazons</u>. Philadelphia: Lippincott, 1931. Illus. by Helene Carter. Grades 6-8.

Seafaring father cryptically cables permission for the four eldest Walker children to spend an adventurous amphibious summer vacation on an "uninhabited" island in the English Lake Country, sailing their own craft Swallow, while Mother and baby remain on the mainland. At war with, or in league with, the rival Amazon pirates, an equally nautical pair of sisters, they subdue unfriendly natives (adults), peacefully co-exist with the friendly ones, especially Mother, and even ferret out treasure buried by real pirates. Lemonade becomes grog, a family squabble is a full-scale mutiny, and ableseaman Titty emerges the heroine.

198. Rinaldo, C. L. <u>Dark Dreams</u>. New York: Harper and Row, 1974. Grades 5-8.

When 12-year-old Carlo's widowed father leaves him in the care of his grandmother while he embarks for the Pacific in uniform in 1943, the delicate, sensitive boy experiences terrifying nightmares impelled by fear of his weak heart and of the brutal bully and his two cohorts who prowl the alley. The mentally retarded man across the alley whom everyone fears protects him and they become fast friends, playing happily in an abandoned brewery. When Carlo's suspicious grandmother discovers them, however, she has the unfortunate Joey J committed to an institution. Carlo's fears return, and he wishes he were strong and brave like his father, not fragile like his mother. When disconsolate Joey J escapes, the authorities agree to let him live in peace with his mother provided he commits no violence, but when the hooligan attacks Carlo with a knife, Joey J instinctively charges to his friend's rescue, is remanded to the asylum, and dies shortly afterward. From his grandmother and his father's letters, Carlo learns revealing things about both his parents' courage.

199. Sonneborn, Ruth A. <u>Friday Night Is Papa Night.</u> New York: Viking Press, 1970. Illus. by Emily A. McCully. Grades K-2.

Papa moonlights to make a living for Mama, Manuela, Carlos, Ricardo and little Pedro and comes home only on Friday nights. One Friday all the preparations are made for Papa's homecoming, but he is delayed. The family eats dinner and still he has not come. Pedro is reluctant to go to sleep in his bed in the kitchen for fear he will miss the anticipated arrival. He awakens late at night when the apartment is dark and looks out the window. The dark shadow he sees is Papa, and Pedro is the only one awake to turn on the light and greet him. The rest of the family stirs, Papa's dinner is reheated, he distributes the presents he's brought, and it's "just like Christmas," says Pedro.

200. Taylor, Sydney. <u>A Papa Like Everyone Else.</u> Chicago: Follett, 1966. Illus. by George Porter. Grades 4-6.

Papa left Hungary for America in 1914, intending to send for Mama and the girls within a year, but the World War and the influenza epidemic delayed his plan for five full years. Mama and Szerena, who is old enough to remember Papa fondly, are eager to join him in a better life in America. Gisella, who was only 1 when he left, does not want to leave her familiar homeland and friends. In the meantime they must continue to operate their humble subsistence farm, raising geese, flax, silkworms and plums. They also relish traditional Jewish and Slovakian festivals and holidays, suffer the depredations of marauding gypsies and foxes, and savor folk food and fairy tales. When Papa finally forwards tickets for their passage, they must soberly face the upheaval of leave-taking and stalwartly meet the challenge and adventure of technology, an ocean voyage, and alien cultures.

201. Van Stockum, Hilda. <u>The Mitchells.</u> New York: Viking Press, 1945. Illus. by the author. Grades 5-6.

Daddy's parting admonition to 10-year-old Joan, eldest of the five Mitchells, as he entrains for the war is not to fill the house with animals in his absence, especially dogs. The ebullient and imaginative youngsters form a club to forestall boredom during the summer but have to vacate their clubhouse when a fractious boy moves to the neighborhood with his mother and an orphaned European refugee, Una, whom the children befriend. Mother decides to take a boarder, but the first one is incompatible with lively scamps and departs hastily with their help, to be replaced by a sprightly old Englishman, Mr. Spencer. Uncle Jim, an airman, comes for Christmas, bearing gifts, but the best part of the holidays is the discovery that moppet Una is Mr. Spencer's long-lost granddaughter Eunice. Word comes that Daddy is lost at sea and joy turns to gloom. Exultation reigns once more when it is learned that Uncle Jim has miraculously saved him. Daddy comes home on leave bringing with him a dog, the sole companion of his ordeal at sea. The children have acquired five stray pets of their own.

202. Yep, Laurence. <u>Dragonwings</u>. New York: Harper and Row, 1975. Grades 7-9.

Moon Shadow is only 8 when he is reluctantly sent by his mother from their home in China to join his father and the other male family members in California, the Land of the Golden Mountain, where they are earning money to send to their families back home by working first on the railroad, later at trades in San Francisco's Chinatown. Moon Shadow's father had been a master kite builder at home, but in America he helps in the family laundry enterprise. A dream reveals to him that in another incarnation he had been physician to the Dragon King himself with the ability to fly, and he longs to fulfill his destiny. Events following the San Francisco earthquake plus his innate mechanical ability polarize his ambition, and he and the boy leave the family establishment to build Dragonwings, a biplane inspired by the Wright brothers. Over the course of seven years they make firm friends with an American couple with whom they exchange cultural traditions, and finally are able to send for Moon Shadow's mother.

Bibliography

199. Sonneborn, Ruth A. <u>Friday Night Is Papa Night.</u> New York: Viking Press, 1970. Illus. by Emily A. McCully. Grades K-2.

    Papa moonlights to make a living for Mama, Manuela, Carlos, Ricardo and little Pedro and comes home only on Friday nights. One Friday all the preparations are made for Papa's homecoming, but he is delayed. The family eats dinner and still he has not come. Pedro is reluctant to go to sleep in his bed in the kitchen for fear he will miss the anticipated arrival. He awakens late at night when the apartment is dark and looks out the window. The dark shadow he sees is Papa, and Pedro is the only one awake to turn on the light and greet him. The rest of the family stirs, Papa's dinner is reheated, he distributes the presents he's brought, and it's "just like Christmas," says Pedro.

200. Taylor, Sydney. <u>A Papa Like Everyone Else.</u> Chicago: Follett, 1966. Illus. by George Porter. Grades 4-6.

    Papa left Hungary for America in 1914, intending to send for Mama and the girls within a year, but the World War and the influenza epidemic delayed his plan for five full years. Mama and Szerena, who is old enough to remember Papa fondly, are eager to join him in a better life in America. Gisella, who was only 1 when he left, does not want to leave her familiar homeland and friends. In the meantime they must continue to operate their humble subsistence farm, raising geese, flax, silkworms and plums. They also relish traditional Jewish and Slovakian festivals and holidays, suffer the depredations of marauding gypsies and foxes, and savor folk food and fairy tales. When Papa finally forwards tickets for their passage, they must soberly face the upheaval of leave-taking and stalwartly meet the challenge and adventure of technology, an ocean voyage, and alien cultures.

201. Van Stockum, Hilda. <u>The Mitchells.</u> New York: Viking Press, 1945. Illus. by the author. Grades 5-6.

    Daddy's parting admonition to 10-year-old Joan, eldest of the five Mitchells, as he entrains for the war is not to fill the house with animals in his absence, especially dogs. The ebullient and imaginative youngsters form a club to forestall boredom during the summer but have to vacate their clubhouse when a fractious boy moves to the neighborhood with his mother and an orphaned European refugee, Una, whom the children befriend. Mother decides to take a boarder, but the first one is incompatible with lively scamps and departs hastily with their help, to be replaced by a sprightly old Englishman, Mr. Spencer. Uncle Jim, an airman, comes for Christmas, bearing gifts, but the best part of the holidays is the discovery that moppet Una is Mr. Spencer's long-lost granddaughter Eunice. Word comes that Daddy is lost at sea and joy turns to gloom. Exultation reigns once more when it is learned that Uncle Jim has miraculously saved him. Daddy comes home on leave bringing with him a dog, the sole companion of his ordeal at sea. The children have acquired five stray pets of their own.

202. Yep, Laurence. Dragonwings. New York: Harper and Row, 1975. Grades 7-9.
Moon Shadow is only 8 when he is reluctantly sent by his mother from their home in China to join his father and the other male family members in California, the Land of the Golden Mountain, where they are earning money to send to their families back home by working first on the railroad, later at trades in San Francisco's Chinatown. Moon Shadow's father had been a master kite builder at home, but in America he helps in the family laundry enterprise. A dream reveals to him that in another incarnation he had been physician to the Dragon King himself with the ability to fly, and he longs to fulfill his destiny. Events following the San Francisco earthquake plus his innate mechanical ability polarize his ambition, and he and the boy leave the family establishment to build Dragonwings, a biplane inspired by the Wright brothers. Over the course of seven years they make firm friends with an American couple with whom they exchange cultural traditions, and finally are able to send for Moon Shadow's mother.

UNWED/INDETERMINABLE

203. Bennett, Anna Elizabeth. Little Witch. Philadelphia: J. B. Lippincott, 1953. Illus. by Lisl Weil. Grades 4-6.

    Nine-year-old Minikin's mother, Madam Snickasnee, is a real witch, the wicked kind who brews black magic, changes children into potted plants, flies about on her broomstick at night, sleeps all day, and screams dire imprecations at her timid, unwitchlike daughter. Little Minx hates being a witch's child; the only magic she ever attempts is clandestinely conjuring up a good fairy, at which she is spectacularly unsuccessful. One day when her mother is safely asleep, she creeps away to enroll herself in school and makes the first friend she has ever had. When a detective comes snooping to find the missing children Madam Snickasnee has enchanted, Minx and her new friends create a potion restoring them to normal, but when her mother discovers the absence of the flower pots, she tries to make Minx's friends into replacements, and she and Minx land in jail. At the witchcraft trial, Madam Snickasnee inadvertently turns herself into an anteater, breaking the evil spell, and Minx learns who her true mother is. Of her old life Minx retains only her magic broomstick.

204. Brelis, Nancy. The Mummy Market. New York: Harper and Row, 1966. Illus. by Ben Schecter. Grades 4-6.

    The Martin children, Elizabeth, 11, Jenny, 10, and Harry, 6, are cared for by the acrimonious housekeeper they call The Gloom. Unable to endure her stifling rules and regulations any longer, they appeal to old Mrs. Cavour, whose fabled garden seems enchanted, for occult intervention. She conjures up a "Mummy Market" where unsuitable mothers can be exchanged for more satisfactory models. The Mummy Market consists of stalls where prospective mothers display themselves to their best advantage with the trappings of their trade. The children's first choice is the fretful, squeamish sort who likes to be called Mimsey. The second, who calls herself Mom, has a physical fitness fetish. The third is a permissive child psychology authority who nearly turns the youngsters into juvenile delinquents.

Their fourth and final choice occupies a bare stall with no gimmicks. She wants to start with a clean slate and let herself grow with the children as imagination and circumstance dictate. Here is a real mother they feel comfortable in calling Mummy.

205. Estes, Eleanor. <u>The Hundred Dresses.</u> New York: Harcourt, Brace, 1944. Illus. by Louis Slobodkin. Grades 3-4.

The fashionable girls in Room 13 poke pernicious fun at Wanda Petronski who lives on the wrong side of the tracks, has a funny name, and wears the same faded but clean blue dress to school everyday while claiming to have a hundred at home in her closet. Their ridicule turns to remorse when they learn that Wanda's drawings of 100 dresses have won the school art contest, but they cannot expiate their behavior because Wanda, her brother and father have moved to the city to escape their gibes. Their guilt is finally absolved when Wanda writes a letter to her former classmates at Christmas time, making them gifts of the choicest of her hundred dresses.

206. Gray, Elizabeth Janet. <u>Adam of the Road.</u> New York: Viking Press, 1942. Illus. by Robert Lawson. Grades 5-7.

Roger the minstrel calls for his son Adam, 11, at the abbey school at St. Albans in 1294. On his retired warhorse Bayard he takes him with Sir Edmund's entourage to London for the wedding of the nobleman's daughter. After the wedding all the minstrels are given purses, but Roger loses his at dice, and the horse as well, to another minstrel named Jankin. The boy and his insouciant father are paupers once more who must ply their trade for meals. The villainous Jankin lames Bayard and absconds with Adam's beloved spaniel Nick in the middle of the night. Father and son set off in pursuit but are separated before reaching St. Giles' Fair, commencing a hue and cry that carries them all over England. After numerous adventures, including an encounter with brigands, père, fils, and dog are reunited in Oxford, and Adam forgoes an opportunity to continue his education there in order to follow the road with his father as a proven peripatetic himself.

207. Gripe, Maria. <u>The Night Daddy.</u> New York: Delacorte, 1968. Illus. by Harald Gripe. Translated by Gerry Bothmer. Grades 4-6.

A young writer answers a newspaper advertisement

for sleep-while-you-work night babysitting and discovers his charge to be a lonely, precocious girl whose unwed mother is a nurse on night shift. With his sensitivity and tact, he overcomes the independent child's resentment at having a sitter thrust upon her, and calls her Julia for the month of her birth when she won't divulge her hated real name. They soon become firm friends, along with the Night Daddy's pet owl Smuggler. Together they engage in philosophical discourses over midnight snacks, exchange dreams, share the magical moment of the blooming of an exotic tropical plant, and worry over Smuggler's disappearance. Julia and the Night Daddy, who is also writing a book on rocks and minerals, write alternate chapters of the narrative.

208. Klein, Norma. Mom, the Wolf Man and Me. New York: Pantheon, 1972. Grades 5-7.
Eleven-year-old Brett's unorthodox photographer mother never married her father (Brett doesn't even know who he is--or care to), and both of them like their casual New York lifestyle just fine, although Brett's grandmother has conventional qualms about the arrangement. Brett's friend Evelyn's feelings are diametrically opposite. She wants to have a father, and her divorced mother is a compulsive husband-hunter who keeps house meticulously, cooks regular meals, and dresses exquisitely, but who attempts suicide when her latest matrimonial hope miscarries. Brett and her mother are both immediately attracted to Theo, owner of a Russian wolfhound whom they meet on an assignment, but Brett is afraid that their impending marriage will spoil her relationship with her mother and their autonomy. She is finally persuaded, especially when she is accorded the master bedroom in the new apartment.

209. Schick, Eleanor. City in the Winter. New York: Macmillan, 1970. Illus. by the author. Grades K-2.
Jimmy wakes up in the morning to find that schools are closed because of the blizzard, but his mother must still go to work while he stays at home with Grandma. After breakfast he helps Grandma straighten the apartment and makes a barn out of a cardboard box. He eats his prepacked school lunch as an indoor picnic and feeds the birds bread crumbs on the windowsill. They make a sortie through the snow to the corner grocery for milk but find it closed. Jimmy peels the onions, washes the vegetables, and sets the table for their soup

supper, and recounts the day's events for his mother when she gets home. She tucks him tenderly to bed.

210. Thurber, James. Many Moons. New York: Harcourt, Brace and World, 1943. Illus. by Louis Slobodkin. Grades K-3.

    When 10-year-old Princess Lenore takes to her bed from a "surfeit of raspberry tarts," her worried father, the King, promises her anything. She desires the moon. The King summons the Lord High Chamberlain, the Royal Wizard and the Royal Mathematician, all of whom have procured, conjured and computed various and sundry items for him in the past, but all agree, if not to the consistency of the moon, at least that its size and distance prohibit its procurement. Only the Court Jester considers consulting the Princess about its size, distance and consistency which she describes as being smaller than her thumbnail, no higher than the tree outside her window, and made of gold. The Jester promptly commissions such a trinket from the Royal Goldsmith and the Princess is happy, but now the Royal brains and even the Jester are stumped on how to conceal the real moon when it rises again. They need not have worried; Lenore has a logical explanation for the regeneration of the moon in the sky also.

211. Turkle, Brinton. The Sky Dog. New York: Viking Press, 1969. Illus. by the author. Grades K-2.

    The boy and his mother are vacationing at the beach. In the cloud patterns the boy sees a shaggy white dog in many attitudes and activities. His mother looks and looks but never sees the sky dog. One day when vacationers are beginning to leave for home, the boy finds a real shaggy white dog. The boy insists it is his sky dog, but his mother knows it is someone's lost pet. For weeks the boy and dog play companionably and no one comes to claim it, but then it is time to go home. The policeman suggests that since the beach is practically deserted now, the boy may as well keep it. But the boy knows that Cloudy has been his dog right along.

212. Wibberly, Leonard. Peter Treegate's War. New York: Farrar, Straus, 1960. Grades 5-8.

    Shortly after the battle of Bunker Hill, Peter's natural father sets off in search of ammunition for the colonial forces, and Peter and his firebrand foster father, the MacLaren of Spey, find themselves sentenced to hang for their part in a sanguinary raid on the British. The sentence is commuted to incarceration on a prison ship on which they meet the militant proselyte, Peace of God Manly, make a daring escape, and rescue a cargo of gunpowder while under heavy fire. The MacLaren goes home to Carolina, leaving Peter and Peace of God to fight on under Washington at Trenton, until a premonition impels him to seek out his foster father, renouncing his natural father to do so. With Peace of God to accompany him, he returns to the scene of his boyhood, only to find that the vengeful MacLaren is embroiled in a brutal, retaliatory feud which Peter cannot endorse. Upon returning North and hearing the bizarre tale of a surrendering British officer, he seeks the blessing of his natural father.

213. Wilkinson, Brenda. Ludell. New York: Harper and Row, 1975. Grades 6-8.

Growing up poor in the segregated South holds its share of rewards for Ludell who has lived with her grandmother, whom she calls Mama, since birth when her unwed mother ran off to New York to take a live-in service position. Her grandmother does day work to support them, and there isn't much loose cash for frills, but Ludell and her irrepressible friends manage to share lighthearted fun, endure embarrassing moments, make occasional mischief, and take adversity in stride. The narrative follows her from the fifth grade with boys teasing girls through the seventh grade with boys getting serious about girls under the watchful eye of "Mama," describing her personal nadirs and zeniths at school, Sunday School picnics, picking cotton, celebrating Christmas, hoping for a TV set, washing the laundry out-of-doors, and just fooling around. An encomium to the dignity and reality of the life of blacks in the South at midcentury told in lyrical patois.

214. Wrightson, Patricia. A Racecourse for Andy. New York: Harcourt, Brace and World, 1968. Illus. by Margaret Horder. Grades 5-6.

The circle of five friends plays a sort of verbal Monopoly in their Sydney suburb, claiming and swapping properties around town. Mentally retarded Andy, 12, does not comprehend the sporting nature of the game, and when an old wino offers to sell him Beecham Park racetrack for three dollars, he liquidates his hard-earned savings to buy it in good faith. His friends try to let him down gently, but his bubble refuses to burst. He takes a more and more proprietary interest in his investment, helping with the gardening and sweeping. The caretakers, concessionaires, horse and dog trainers, and patrons indulge the boy, encouraging his harmless fiction, until he becomes a celebrity. When he begins painting bleachers, tampering with the mechanical hare, letting stray dogs loose inside, and decorating with streamers, the actual owners take a dim view and offer to buy it back from him. Andy turns a tidy profit and is none the wiser.

215. Zolotow, Charlotte. *The Summer Night*. New York: Harper and Row, 1974. Illus. by Ben Shecter. Grades K-2.

The little girl's father cares for her all day and in the evening bathes her and puts her to bed, but she isn't sleepy. He brings her a glass of water and an apple, and opens the window to the soft night air, but still she isn't drowsy. In sympathetic understanding he carries her downstairs, reads her a story and plays her a nocturne, but they don't produce slumber. He takes her for a walk in the dark garden with fireflies, rabbits, and the moon reflected in the pond. An owl hoots as they go inside for warm milk and bread. He carries her up and tucks her in tenderly, and when the owl hoots again she doesn't hear it because she is sound asleep.

VI

APPENDIX:
AUDIOVISUAL MATERIAL

The following annotated compilation of films, filmstrips, videotapes, audio tapes, kits, slides, pictures, and transparencies, as well as a few germane periodical articles and nonfiction books, was conceived as a useful adjunct to the basic list of 215 works of children's fiction on which the detailed analysis was performed. An effort was made to locate multimedia materials for primary and intermediate children, as well as for junior and senior high youths, but the available offerings for elementary grades remains small in this still controversial subject area.

The compilation is divided into the following categories:

Filmstrips	Pictures
Kit	Model (puppets)
Microform	Slides
Motion pictures	Audio tapes
Articles	Videotapes
and books	Transparencies

At the end of this listing appears distributors' addresses.

FILMSTRIPS

<u>Broken Homes and Families</u>. Los Angeles, Family Films, 1970. Dist. by Society for Visual Education. 1 filmstrip, color; 1 disc recording. Age level: junior high, high school.

Presents teens discussing the pressures and problems of broken homes and how to overcome the handicaps.

Death: A Part of Life. New York, Guidance Associates, 1978. Dist. by producer. 2 filmstrips, black and white, 2 disc recordings or cassettes, discussion guide. Age level: intermediate.

Part I presents in easily understandable language the processes of denial, acceptance and readjustment as normal, universal experiences. Part II comprises a sensitively visualized case history narrated by a young girl whose father died a year ago.

Families in Crisis. S. A. Films, no date. Dist. by Coronet. 8 filmstrips, black & white; 4 cassettes. Age level: junior high, high school.

These case studies of problems in family living offer alternatives and open up questions on divorce, coping with death, a brush with the law, pulling up roots, care of the aged and handicapped, etc.

The Family Circle. Pasadena, Calif., Barr Films, 1978. Dist. by producer. 4 filmstrips, color, 4 cassettes, teacher's guide. Age level: junior high, high school.

"The Normal Family" discusses siblings, role-playing, unresolved conflicts, individual differences. "The Divorced Family" examines guilt and resentment, step-relationships, growth and strength. "The Adoptive Family" deals with the many problems of adoption. "Death in the Family" views terminal illness, sudden death, interfamilial support, coping with loss.

Understanding Changes in the Family. New York, Guidance Associates, no date. Dist. by producer. 5 filmstrips, color, 5 disc recordings or cassettes, discussion guide. Age level: pre-school, primary.

"What's a Family?" examines roles of children, parents, other adults; emphasizes family cooperation. "Little Brother, Big Pest!" dramatizes ways young siblings can cause jealousy, feelings of parental rejection. "We're Adopted!" explains what adoption is, why it happens. "Not Together Anymore" focuses on reasons for divorce, children's reactions, ways for children to adjust. "Playing Dead" articulates common fears and questions about death through peer conversation.

Audiovisual Material

When Two Divide. Shawnee Mission, Kans., Marshfilm, 1977. Dist. by the producer. 1 filmstrip, color; 1 disc or cassette recording, teacher's guide. Age level: primary, intermediate.

A realistic, thoughtful and warm look at new forms of families developed as a result of divorce, focusing on the child and his ability to cope with divorce in his family; suggesting to the student healthy outlets for frustrations and acceptable modes of behavior. Imagination and humor make the usually heavy subject both interesting and informative. Received the Bronze Award of the New York International Film Festival.

Your Family. Boulder, Colo. Learning Tree Filmstrips, 1974. Dist. by the producer. 4 filmstrips, color; 2 cassettes, teacher's guide. Age level: intermediate.

Prepared to enforce the viewer from a broken home, this series demonstrates the progression from infancy to old age and family members' interrelationships under varying family situations, including divorce, death, and illness.

KIT

Schools, Families, Neighborhoods. Chicago, Field Enterprises, 1969. Dist. by the producer. 39 posters, 9 shortstrips, 3 disc recordings, 4 charts, 3 scripts, 3 filmstrips, teacher's manual. Age level: primary.

Presents all aspects of family living, conflict, and change from the advent of a new baby to a grandparent coming to live in the home, sibling rivalry, working mothers, and father absent.

MICROFORM

Grover. Ann Arbor, Mich. Xedia Micromedia Classroom Libraries, no date. Dist. by the producer. 2 microfiche, 4 x 6, black & white. Age level: intermediate, junior high.

Grover's terminally ill mother takes her own life, plunging his father into open, uncomprehending anguish, while Grover suffers silently, attempting to plumb the unfathomable depths of mortality.

MOTION PICTURES

<u>Death: Coping with Loss</u>. Chicago, Coronet, no date. Dist. by the producer. 16 mm., color. Age level: junior high, high school.

 Real people look squarely into the face of a deep personal experience: families with recent grief still fresh in their memory, young people whose vision of death has been fashioned in the cosmetic image of the TV screen, victims of illness facing imminent death.

<u>A Family for Now</u>. New York, Jewish Child Care Assoc., 1965. Currently out-of-print; formerly dist. by Harvest Films. 16 mm., black & white. Age level: intermediate, junior high.

 Tells the story of a 9-year-old boy who becomes the innocent victim of a broken home and feels the impact of his father's desertion and his mother's nervous breakdown. Describes how he adjusts when placed in a foster home where he is given the love and attention he needs.

<u>What Fixed Me</u>. American Film Institute, no date. Dist. by Time Life Films Multimedia Division. 16 mm., color, 20 min. Age level: high school.
 Film centers on a boy's fight to free himself from his domineering ex-preacher father after his mother's suicide. The incidents are largely viewed through the boy's eyes and in flashbacks that add another dimension of consciousness and interest.

ARTICLES AND BOOKS (by Author)

DeLeeuw, Adele. "Dad Is Gone...," <u>Young Miss</u>, July 1974, p. 52-59. Age level: junior high.

 A story about the death of a parent.

Demarest, V. "How to Handle Your Parents' Divorce," <u>Young Miss</u>, March 1973, p. 38-42. Age level: junior high.

 [Not inspected.]

Educational Research Council of America. "Handling Feelings

of Anger" (pamphlet). Book V of "Why People Act As They Do" series. Cleveland: The Council, 1972. 26 pages, illustrations. Age level: intermediate.

When Martha's mother died and her father couldn't raise her by himself, she was given to her aunt to rear. Left alone all day, she is desperately lonely. She tries all kinds of attention-getting devices but nothing seems to work.

Gardner, Richard A. The Boys and Girls Book About Divorce. New York: Science House, 1970. 159 pages, illustrations. Age level: intermediate.

The author draws on 13 years' experience as a child psychiatrist; the book is frank and honest and fills the needs of providing children with valid information and guidance for dealing with various divorce situations.

Hatch, C. "My Parents Are Divorced," Co-Ed, January 1972, p. 11-12. Age level: junior high, high school.

[Not inspected.]

LeShan, Eda. Learning to Say Good-By: When a Parent Dies. New York: Macmillan, 1976. 85 pages, illustrations, bibliography. Age level: intermediate.

Book is written in a reassuring tone, encouraging the survivors to help each other share the burden of grief. All the situations presented involve conventional two-parent families in which one dies. Remarriage is discussed.

Pfeffer, Susan Beth. "The Semi-Step-Daughter," American Girl, December 1973, p. 29. Age level: intermediate, junior high.

Laurie lives with her divorced mother but must visit her father and his new wife at Christmas vacation and wonders how to get along with her stepmother for two whole weeks.

Richards, Arlene, and Irene Willis. How to Get It Together When Your Parents Are Coming Part. New York: David McKay, 1976. 170 pages. Age level: junior high, high school.

Tells adolescents which parts of a divorce concern

them and what they can do about them, which parts do not concern them and how to stay out of them, how to get help if they feel more is happening than they can handle alone, and how to build their own lives no matter what parents do with theirs.

PICTURES

<u>Living with Dying.</u> Mt. Dora, Fla., Documentary Photo Aids, no date. Dist. by the producer. 24 prints, 11 x 14, black & white, teacher's guide. Age level: junior high, high school.

This series explores the vital issues confronting a society oriented against death as a natural process, how to comfort the dying family member, how the survivors should deal with grief, etc.

MODEL

<u>Black Family Hand Puppets.</u> Philadelphia, Life-Like Hand Puppets, no date. Dist. by the producer. 5 puppets, 12 - 14 inches. Age level: primary, intermediate.

Consists of father, mother, teenager and two younger siblings and is designed to promote the interpretation and articulation of emotion and personality. Two puppets can be operated simultaneously to extemporize dialogue and dramatize situations.

SLIDES

<u>Living with Dying.</u> Sunburst Communications, 1974. Dist. by the Center for the Humanities. 155 slides, 2 carousel cartridges, 2 cassettes, 2 disc recordings, teacher's guide. Age level: junior high, high school.

Students study the various reasons for our fear of death and see how we attempt to deny death by searching for some sort of immortality. The psychological stages of the terminally ill are examined.

AUDIO TAPES

Life Without Father. WSUI Radio, State University of Iowa, 1966. Dist. by National Tape Repository. 1 tape, 3-3/4 ips, 1-track. Age level: junior high, high school.

This tape is one of the How's the Family Series that emphasizes the importance of the family to its members and to the society of which it is a part.

VIDEOTAPES

Breakup. Bloomington, Ind., National Instructional TV Center, 1973. Dist. by the producer. 1 cassette, 3/4 in., color, 14 min., 43 sec. Age level: intermediate.

Presents Becky whose feelings of guilt, loneliness, anger and fear are stirred up as she anticipates a visit by her father who is separated from her mother. Follows her emotions as she imagines the frightening consequences of divorce.

The Bridge of Adam Rush. Paramus, N. J., Time Life Films Multimedia Division, no date. Dist. by the producer. 1 tape, flexible format, color, 47 min. Age level: junior high.

The sensitive and moving story of a 12-year-old's struggle to win the love of his new stepfather and adjust to the hardships of farm life in the early 1800's after his father's sudden death and disruption of his comfortable and happy urban life.

TRANSPARENCIES

Family Relations--The One-Parent Family--A Series. Big Spring, Texas, Creative Visuals, Inc., 1968. Dist. by the producer. 4 sets, 9 x 11, color. Age level: junior high.

Explores the causes of the single parent family and depicts the mother-absent and father-absent white families, and the father-absent black family.

DISTRIBUTORS' ADDRESSES

Barr Films
P. O. Box 5667
Pasadena, Calif.   91107

The Center for the Humanities
2 Holland Ave.
White Plains, N. Y.   10603

Coronet
65 E. South Water St.
Chicago, Ill.   60601

Creative Visuals, Inc.
P. O. Box 1911
Big Spring, Texas   79720

Documentary Photo Aids
P. O. Box 956
Mt. Dora, Fla.   32757

Field Enterprises Educational Corp.
School and Library Services
510 Merchandise Mart Plaza
Chicago, Ill.   60654

Guidance Associates
757 Third Ave.
New York, N. Y.   10017

Harvest Films
309 Fifth Ave.
New York, N. Y.   10036

Learning Tree Filmstrips
934 Pearl St., Box 1590,
   Dept. 25OA
Boulder, Colo.   80302

Life-Like Hand Puppets
611 Colebrook Dr.
Philadelphia, Pa.   19115

Marshfilm
P. O. Box 8082
Shawnee Mission, Kans.
   66208

National Instructional TV
   Center
11 W. 17th St., Box A
Bloomington, Ind.   47401

National Tape Repository
University of Colorado
Boulder, Colo.   80302

Society for Visual Education
1345 Diversey Parkway
Chicago, Ill.   60614

Time Life Films Multimedia
   Division
100 Eisenhower Dr.
Paramus, N. J.   07652

Xedia Micromedia Classroom
   Libraries
300 N. Zeeb Rd.
Ann Arbor, Mich.   48106

INDEX
(to the Bibliography)
BY PREDOMINANT PARENT
(showing titles and citing entry numbers)

MOTHER

Angelo (The Bells of Bleecker Street) 183
Angelo (Nino) 184
Armstrong (Sounder) 185

Barber (The Ghosts) 1
Barnwell (Shadow on the Water) 97
Beatty (Me, California Perkins) 99
Beckett (My Brother Angel) 3
Benary-Isbert (The Ark) 187
Bennett (Little Witch) 203
Bishop (Pancakes-Paris) 4
Blue (A Month of Sundays) 100
Blume (It's Not the End of the World) 101
Bradbury (Boy on the Run) 102
Bradley (Meeting with a Stranger) 188
Brelis (The Mummy Market) 204
Bulla (Open the Door and See All the People) 8
Burch (Queenie Peavy) 189
Burglon (Sticks Across the Chimney) 9

Cameron (A Room Made of Windows) 12
Carlson (The Family Under the Bridge) 13
Cavanna (A Touch of Magic) 15
Coblentz (Martin and Abraham Lincoln) 191
Cohen (Thank You, Jackie Robinson) 21
Cookson (The Nipper) 23
Corcoran (Axe-Time/Sword-Time) 105

Daringer (Like a Lady) 27
DeAngeli (The Lion in the Box) 29
Donovan (I'll Get There. It Better Be Worth the Trip) 108

Index by Predominant Parent

(MOTHER continued)

Doty (Gabriel) 30
Duncan (Down a Dark Hall) 31
Duncan (A Gift of Magic) 109

Edmonds (Two Logs Crossing) 32
Estes (The Moffats) 37
Estes (The Middle Moffat) 38
Estes (Rufus M.) 39
Ewing (A Private Matter) 111
Eyerly (The World of Ellen March) 112

Farjeon (Maria Lupin) 194
Farley (The Garden Is Doing Fine) 41
Fox (How Many Miles to Babylon) 114
Fox (Blowfish Live in the Sea) 115
Fox (The Slave Dancer) 45
Freuchen (Eskimo Boy) 46

Goff (Where Is Daddy? The Story of a Divorce) 116
Gray (Jane Hope) 49
Gray (Star Bright) 50
Gray (Star Lost) 51
Greene (A Girl Called Al) 117
Greene (I Know You, Al) 118
Greenfield (Sister) 52
Gripe (The Night Daddy) 207

Hegan (Mrs. Wiggs of the Cabbage Patch) 54
Heide (When the Sad One Comes to Stay) 119
Heide (Growing Anyway Up) 55
Holland (Heads You Win; Tails I Lose) 120
Hunter (A Sound of Chariots) 57

Johnson (The Grizzly) 121

Kerr (Love Is a Missing Person) 122
Klein (It's Not What You Expect) 123
Klein (Mom, the Wolf Man and Me) 208
Klein (Taking Sides) 124
Klein (What It's All About) 125

Lampman (The Shy Stegosaurus of Cricket Creek) 60
L'Engle (A Wrinkle in Time) 196
Lewis (Young Fu of the Upper Yangtze) 61
Lexau (Emily and the Klunky Baby and the Next-Door Dog 126

Index by Predominant Parent

(MOTHER continued)

Lexau (Me Day) 127
Lisker (Two Special Cards) 128

Madison (Marinka, Katinka and Me [Susie]) 62
Mann (My Dad Lives in a Downtown Hotel) 129
Mathis (Listen for the Fig Tree) 63
Meigs (Wind in the Chimney) 64
Moon (Chi-Wee) 65

Neville (Garden of Broken Glass) 131
Newfield (A Book for Jodan) 132
Norris (Lillan) 133

Peck (Don't Look and It Won't Hurt) 134
Pfeffer (The Beauty Queen) 136
Platt (The Boy Who Could Make Himself Disappear) 138
Platt (Chloris and the Creeps) 139
Platt (Chloris and the Freaks) 140

Ransome (Swallows and Amazons) 197

Sachs (The Bears' House) 141
Sawyer (The Year of Jubilo) 71
Schick (City in the Winter) 209
Shannon (Dobry) 72
Sidney (Five Little Peppers) 73
Slote (Matt Gargan's Boy) 142
Smith (Tough Chauncey) 143
Snyder (First Step) 144
Sonneborn (Friday Night Is Papa Night) 199
Stolz (Leap Before You Look) 146

Taylor (A Papa Like Everyone Else) 200
Taylor (Teetoncey) 82
Taylor (Teetoncey and Ben O'Neal) 83
Thomas (Eliza's Daddy) 147
Turkle (The Sky Dog) 211

Ullman (Banner in the Sky) 84

Van Stockum (The Mitchells) 201

Wagner (J. T.) 148
Walter (Lillie of Watts) 86
Wayne (The Witches of Barguzin) 87

Index by Predominant Parent

(MOTHER continued)

Webb   (Quest of the Otter)   88
Wojciechowska   (Shadow of a Bull)   95
Wolitzer   (Out of Love)   149
Wrightson   (A Racecourse for Andy)   214

Zolotow   (A Father Like That)   150

FATHER

Alexander   (To Live a Lie)   96

Bawden   (Three on the Run)   2
Bond   (A String in the Harp)   5
Bragdon   (There Is a Tide)   6
Brink   (Winter Cottage)   7
Burnett   (A Little Princess)   10

Cavanna   (Love, Laurie)   14
Christopher   (The Prince in Waiting)   16
Cleaver   (Ellen Grae)   103
Cleaver   (Lady Ellen Grae)   104
Cleaver   (The Mimosa Tree)   17
Cleaver   (Grover)   18
Cleaver   (I Would Rather Be a Turnip)   19
Collier   (Give Dad My Best)   192
Constant   (Those Miller Girls!)   22
Corcoran   (Sasha My Friend)   24
Corcoran   (The Winds of Time)   193

Dahl   (Danny the Champion of the World)   25
Daringer   (Bigity Anne)   26
Daringer   (Stepsister Sally)   28

Enright   (The Saturdays)   33
Enright   (The Four Story Mistake)   34
Enright   (Then There Were Five)   35
Enright   (Spiderweb for Two)   36
Estes   (The Hundred Dresses)   205

Faber   (Cathy at the Crossroads)   40
Flory   (The Golden Venture)   43
Fox   (Portrait of Ivan)   44

Garfield   (Devil in the Fog)   47
Gray   (Adam of the Road)   206

(FATHER continued)

Harnett   (The Great House)   53

Johnson   (The Black Symbol)   58
Johnson   (A Golden Touch)   59

Klein   (Taking Sides)   124

Mazer   (Guy Lenny)   130

Nash   (While Mrs. Coverlet Was Away)   66
Ness   (Sam, Bangs and Moonshine)   67

Ormondroyd   (Time at the Top)   68
Ormondroyd   (All in Good Time)   69

Perl   (The Telltale Summer of Tina C.)   135
Pfeffer   (Marly the Kid)   137
Polland   (The White Twilight)   70

Snyder   (Eyes in the Fishbowl)   145
Sperry   (Call it Courage)   75
Spykman   (A Lemon and a Star)   76
Steele   (Winter Danger)   77
Steele   (The Year of the Bloody Sevens)   78
Stephens   (Witch of the Cumberlands)   79
Stolz   (The Edge of Next Year)   80

Talbot   (Away Is So Far)   81
Thurber   (Many Moons)   210

Voight   (Apple Tree Cottage)   85

Weber   (Meet the Malones)   89
Weber   (Beany Malone)   90
Wellman   (The Wilderness Has Ears)   91
Whitehead   (The Mother Tree)   92
Wibberly   (Peter Treegate's War)   212
Williams   (Oh, Susanna!)   93
Wojciechowska   ("Hey, What's Wrong with This One?")   94

Yep   (Dragonwings)   202

Zolotow   (The Summer Night)   215

Index by Predominant Parent

GRANDMOTHER

Alexander (Trouble on Treat Street) 151

Clymer (My Brother Stevie) 20
Corcoran (This Is a Recording) 107

Fenton (Duffy's Rocks) 42
Fitzhugh (The Long Secret) 113

Kleberger (Traveling with Oma) 195

Lampman (Navaho Sister) 166
Lexau (Benjie) 168
Lexau (Benjie On His Own) 169

Means (Shuttered Windows) 171

Rinaldo (Dark Dreams) 198

Shotwell (Magdalena) 174
Snyder (The Egypt Game) 74

Wier (The Barrel) 179
Wilkinson (Ludell) 213

AUNT

Anckarsvard (Aunt Vinnie's Invasion) 181
Anckarsvard (Aunt Vinnie's Victorious Six) 182
Bawden (The House of Secrets) 186
Byars (The Summer of the Swans) 11
Hunt (Up a Road Slowly) 56
O'Dell (Zia) 172
Talbot (A Home With Aunt Florry) 177

UNCLE

Bellairs (The Figure in the Shadows) 153
Burnett (The Secret Garden) 157
Fleischman (Chancy and the Grand Rascal) 162
Gage (Big Blue Island) 164
Goudge (Linnets and Valerians) 48
Lawrence (Peachtree Island) 167
Pope (The Sherwood Ring) 173
Van Stockum (Andries) 178

GRANDFATHER

Byars   (After the Goat Man)   158
Lampman   (The Shy Stegosaurus of Indian Springs)   166
Spyri   (Heidi)   175

SISTER

Cleaver   (Where the Lilies Bloom)   160

UNRELATED FEMALE

Bauer   (Shelter From the Wind)   98
Bawden   (The Witch's Daughter)   152
Burch   (Skinny)   156
Carlson   (Ann Aurelia and Dorothy)   190
Corcoran   (A Dance to Still Music)   106
Dunnahoo   (Who Cares About Espie Sanchez?)   110
Flory   (Faraway Dream)   163
Wier   (The Loner)   180

UNRELATED MALE

Bragdon   (That Jud!)   154
Bulla   (White Bird)   155
Clark   (Secret of the Andes)   159
Cunningham   (Dorp Dead)   161
Lindgren   (Rasmus and the Vagabond)   170
Streatfeild   (The Children on the Top Floor)   176

AUTHOR INDEX
(to the Bibliography;
citing entry numbers)

Alexander, Anne 96, 151
Anckarsvard, Karin 181, 182
Angelo, Valenti 183, 184
Armstrong, William H. 185
Barber, Antonia 1
Barnwell, Robinson 97
Bauer, Marion Dane 98
Bawden, Nina 2, 152, 186
Beatty, Patricia 99
Beckett, Hilary 3
Bellairs, John 153
Benary-Isbert, Margot 187
Bennett, Anna Elizabeth 203
Bishop, Claire Hutchet 4
Blue, Rose 100
Blume, Judy 101
Bond, Nancy 5
Bradbury, Bianca 102
Bradley, Duane 188
Bragdon, Elspeth 6, 154
Brelis, Nancy 204
Brink, Carol Ryrie 7
Bulla, Clyde Robert 8, 155
Burch, Robert 156, 189
Burglon, Nora 9
Burnett, Frances Hodgson 10, 157
Byars, Betsy 11, 158
Cameron, Eleanor 12
Carlson, Natalie Savage 13, 190
Cavanna, Betty 14, 15
Christopher, John 16
Clark, Ann Nolan 159

Cleaver, Bill 17, 18, 19, 103, 104, 160
Cleaver, Vera 17, 18, 19, 103, 104, 160
Clymer, Eleanor 20
Coblentz, Catherine Cate 191
Cohen, Barbara 21
Collier, James Lincoln 192
Constant, Alberta Wilson 22
Cookson, Catherine 23
Corcoran, Barbara 24, 105, 106, 107, 193
Cunningham, Julia 161
Dahl, Roald 25
Daringer, Helen F. 26, 27, 28
Dean, Leigh 128
DeAngeli, Marguerite 29
Donovan, John 108
Doty, Jean Slaughter 30
Duncan, Lois 31, 109
Dunnahoo, Terry 110
Edmonds, Walter D. 32
Enright, Elizabeth 33, 34, 35, 36
Estes, Eleanor 37, 38, 39, 205
Ewing, Kathryn 111
Eyerly, Jeannette 112
Faber, Nancy W. 40
Farjeon, Annabel 194
Farley, Carol 41
Fenton, Edward 42

Author Index

Fitzhugh, Louise 113
Fleischman, Sid 162
Flory, Jane 43, 163
Fox, Paula 44, 45, 114, 115
Freuchen, Pipaluk 46
Gage, Wilson 164
Garfield, Leon 47
Goff, Beth 116
Goudge, Elizabeth 48
Gray, Elizabeth Janet 49, 206
Gray, Patsey 50, 51
Greene, Constance C. 117, 118
Greenfield, Eloise 52
Gripe, Maria 207
Harnett, Cynthia 53
Hegan, Alice Caldwell 54
Heide, Florence Parry 55, 119
Holland, Isabelle 120
Hunt, Irene 56
Hunter, Mollie 57
Johnson, Annabel 58, 59, 121
Johnson, Edgar 58, 59, 121
Kerr, M. E. 122
Kleberger, Ilse 195
Klein, Norma 123, 124, 125, 208
Lampman, Evelyn Sibley 60, 165, 166
Lawrence, Mildred 167
L'Engle, Madeleine 196
Lewis, Elizabeth Foreman 61
Lexau, Joan M. 126, 127, 168, 169
Lindgren, Astrid 170
Lisker, Sonia O. 128
Madison, Winifred 62
Mann, Peggy 129
Mathis, Sharon Bell 63
Mazer, Harry 130
Means, Florence Crannell 171
Meigs, Cornelia 64
Moon, Grace 65
Nash, Mary 66
Ness, Evaline 67
Neville, Emily Cheney 131
Newfield, Marcia 132
Norris, Gunilla B. 133
O'Dell, Scott 172
Ormondroyd, Edward 68, 69
Peck, Richard 134
Perl, Lila 135
Pfeffer, Susan Beth 136, 137
Platt, Kin 138, 139, 140
Polland, Madeleine 70
Pope, Elizabeth Marie 173
Ransome, Arthur 197
Rinaldo, C. L. 198
Sachs, Marilynn 141
Sawyer, Ruth 71
Schick, Eleanor 209
Shannon, Monica 72
Shotwell, Louisa R. 174
Sidney, Margaret 73
Slote, Alfred 142
Smith, Doris Buchanan 143
Snyder, Anne 144
Snyder, Zilpha Keatley 74, 145
Sonneborn, Ruth A. 199
Sperry, Armstrong 75
Spykman, E. C. 76
Spyri, Johanna 175
Steele, William O. 77, 78
Stephens, Mary Jo 79
Stolz, Mary 80, 146
Streatfeild, Noel 176
Talbot, Charlene Joy 177
Talbot, Toby 81
Taylor, Sydney 200
Taylor, Theodore 82, 83
Thomas, Ianthe 147
Thurber, James 210
Turkle, Brinton 211
Ullman, James Ramsey 84
Van Stockum, Hilda 178, 201
Voight, Virginia F. 85
Wagner, Jane 148
Walter, Mildred Pitts 86
Wayne, Kyra Petrovskaya 87

Webb, Christopher 88
Weber, Lenora Mattingly 89, 90
Wellman, Alice 91
Whitehead, Ruth 92
Wibberly, Leonard 212
Wier, Ester 179, 180
Wilkinson, Brenda 213
Williams, J. R. 93
Wojciechowska, Maia 94, 95
Wolitzer, Hilma 149
Wrightson, Patricia 214
Yep, Laurence 202
Zolotow, Charlotte 150, 215

SUBJECT INDEX
(to the Bibliography; citing entry numbers)

Accidental death 1, 5, 24, 46, 50, 63, 74, 75, 80, 82, 84, 87, 88, 95, 151, 155, 177, 178
Adolescent concerns 11, 14, 49, 56, 80, 83, 84, 90, 93, 98, 104, 108, 118, 120, 123, 124, 130, 135, 146
Alcoholism 56, 63, 80, 115, 120, 131, 144, 156
American Indians 32, 65, 107, 165, 166, 172
American Revolution 15, 173, 212
Angola 91
Apparitions 1, 79, 145, 153, 173
Australia 214

Birthdays 38, 62, 76, 86, 96, 127, 133, 181
Blacks 2, 21, 45, 52, 63, 86, 91, 114, 122, 127, 131, 143, 148, 151, 168, 169, 171, 182, 185, 188, 190, 191, 213
Bulgaria 72

Caldecott medalists 67, 210
California 12, 43, 50, 51, 74, 86, 99, 110, 132, 151, 172, 202
China 61
City stories (U.S.) 3, 8, 15, 17, 20, 29, 33, 42, 100, 108, 110, 114, 117, 118, 119, 125, 127, 129, 130, 131, 138, 141, 145, 148, 151, 158, 168, 169, 174, 177, 183, 208, 209
Civil War 49, 153, 191
Clairvoyance 3, 31, 79, 109, 152
Colorado 193
Conflicting loyalties (divorce) 119, 124, 125, 128, 130, 135
Connecticut 37, 38, 39
Cottage industries 9, 64, 160, 163

Delinquency/incorrigibles 6, 17, 20, 110, 114, 139, 143, 148, 151, 154, 178, 189

Subject Index

Denmark 9, 70
The Depression (1930's) 7, 42, 71, 97, 189, 192
Diaries 52, 107, 207
District of Columbia 52, 191
Divorce stigma 96, 112, 129, 133
Drug Abuse 23
Dying family member/close friend 21, 41, 57, 81, 108, 111, 117, 160

Early twentieth century 22, 29, 37, 38, 39, 48, 54, 57, 61, 76, 87, 92, 157, 184, 200, 202
Eighteenth century 47, 64, 77, 78, 155, 163, 172
Employed mothers (within the home) 9, 15, 21, 30, 37, 38, 39, 45, 50, 51, 60, 64, 65, 187
Employed mothers (outside the home) 8, 23, 27, 29, 62, 74, 86, 99, 100, 101, 106, 111, 116, 117, 118, 119, 124, 133, 134, 139, 142, 148, 189, 207, 208, 209
England 1, 2, 10, 16, 23, 25, 47, 48, 53, 157, 176, 186, 194, 197, 206
Ethiopia 188

Farm/ranch stories 9, 24, 50, 60, 64, 72, 85, 92, 93, 97, 159, 167, 175, 180, 188, 200
Father custody (divorce) 96, 98, 103, 104, 124, 130, 135, 137, 145
Father-daughter conflict 118, 146
Father-son conflict 6, 42, 77, 80, 115, 121, 127, 129, 130, 138, 212
Feminism 99, 167, 208
Foster homes 110, 156, 161, 170, 190
France 4, 13
Frontier stories 32, 77, 78, 93, 155, 162

Games/sports stories 21, 25, 36, 74, 121, 142, 197
Georgia 143, 156, 185, 189
Germany 187, 195
Gold Rush stories 43, 58, 59, 99
Great depression 7, 42, 71, 97, 189, 192
Greenland 46
Guardian-ward conflict 56, 143, 155, 161, 164, 177, 178, 180, 193

Hobbies/vocations 12, 25, 33, 53, 57, 72, 84, 109, 110, 123, 136, 140, 145, 171, 176, 184, 194, 202, 206

Subject Index

Holidays 3, 4, 29, 37, 39, 63, 72, 73, 74, 124, 146, 148, 165, 167, 176, 183, 184, 187, 190, 200, 201, 205, 213
Holland 178
Homosexuality 41
Housekeepers 33, 34, 35, 36, 40, 66, 76, 89, 94, 152, 167, 176, 178, 204
Humorous stories 25, 37, 38, 39, 60, 66, 94, 117, 118, 162, 166, 195, 204, 210
Hungary 200
Hyperbole/prevarication 67, 103, 104, 107

Identity crises 11, 44, 67, 92, 95, 107, 111, 113, 117, 119, 123, 130, 132, 135, 137, 159, 165, 171, 172, 179, 180
Illegitimacy 19, 134, 207, 208, 213
Illinois 17
Immigration/emigration 64, 184, 200, 202
Island Stories 6, 46, 75, 82, 83, 106, 138, 164, 167, 171, 179, 197
Italy 184

Kansas 22, 93, 162
Kentucky 78, 79

Latin Americans 3, 110, 139, 140, 151, 174, 199
Louisiana 45

Maine 6, 71, 154
Massachusetts 115
Mental/emotional illness 55, 102, 138, 141, 186, 192, 193
Midwest 41, 56, 66, 112, 162
Missouri 131
Montana 24, 107, 180
Moral dilemmas 17, 103, 133
Mother-daughter conflict 57, 63, 74, 86, 96, 105, 107, 119, 120, 126, 134, 136, 137, 139, 140, 144, 146, 190, 203
Mother-son conflict 83, 84, 88, 100, 108, 138

New York 3, 20, 21, 29, 33, 100, 102, 108, 114, 125, 135, 138, 139, 140, 173, 177, 183
Newbery medalists 11, 45, 56, 61, 72, 75, 95, 159, 185, 196, 206
Nineteenth century 10, 23, 32, 43, 45, 49, 58, 59, 73, 82,

Subject Index

83, 84, 85, 88, 93, 99, 162, 175
North Carolina 17, 49, 82, 83
Northeast 30, 34, 35, 36, 73, 76, 80, 88, 105, 113, 115, 119, 123, 124, 174

Obesity 117, 120, 153
Oklahoma 98
Orphanages 156, 161, 163, 170
Overcompensation by absent fathers (divorce) 100, 117, 129

Pennsylvania 14, 15, 42, 55, 64, 85, 163, 167
Peru 159
Pet/doll stories 8, 24, 27, 30, 50, 51, 67, 108, 116, 185, 211
Physical handicaps 106, 138, 152
Polynesia 75, 88
Preschool/primary fantasy 210, 211
Preschool/primary realistic stories 67, 116, 126, 127, 128, 132, 147, 148, 150, 168, 169, 199, 209, 215

Quarreling parents 97, 99, 101, 116, 120, 128, 129, 132

Racial mistrust 91, 100, 143, 151, 174, 188, 202, 205
Reconciliation 97, 99, 123
Reconciliation attempts by children 101, 109, 112, 121, 129, 142, 149
Remarriage 12, 22, 23, 28, 31, 32, 43, 49, 56, 65, 69, 74, 93, 94, 98, 102, 106, 109, 111, 113, 115, 118, 122, 125, 130, 133, 135, 137, 139, 140, 142, 146, 147, 149, 178, 190, 208
Remarriage, rebellion to by children 12, 40, 49, 93, 98, 109, 130, 139, 140
Renaissance/Middle Ages 53, 70, 206
Retardation 11, 103, 198, 214
Runaways 2, 19, 98, 101, 102, 106, 110, 112, 122, 137, 143, 155, 161, 170
Russia 87

School stories 10, 20, 27, 31, 62, 96, 100, 103, 120, 137, 138, 141, 144, 166, 171, 174, 185, 190, 205
Science fiction 1, 5, 16, 60, 68, 69, 166, 196
Scotland 57, 152

Subject Index

Sea stories 67, 75, 82, 83, 88
Seasonal stories 7, 24, 34, 53, 71, 77, 92, 126, 160, 215
Self-determinism (by children) 17, 32, 46, 66, 75, 85, 87, 88, 89, 102, 105, 136, 145, 160
Sibling strife 5, 11, 20, 26, 52, 71, 92, 122, 126, 141, 179
Single men as adoptive parents 154, 155, 159, 161, 170, 176
Single women as adoptive parents 152, 156, 163, 180
Social injustice 17, 23, 57, 158
South 19, 44, 54, 122, 160, 213
South Carolina 97, 171
Southwest 65, 165, 166
Spain 81, 95
Stepparent-child conflict 40, 76, 115, 130, 139, 140
Step-sibling strife 28, 147
Suicide 18, 139
Summer vacations 11, 14, 35, 76, 85, 102, 104, 113, 123, 135, 165, 195, 211
Sweden 133, 170, 181, 182, 207
Switzerland 84, 175

Tennessee 155, 164
Texas 92
Thumb sucking 141
Timidity 55, 75, 121, 153, 168, 198

Wales 5
Washington [state] 104
West 60
Wisconsin 7
Witchcraft 48, 79, 153, 203, 204
World War I 39, 57, 200
World War II 4, 34, 35, 41, 89, 90, 105, 183, 187, 198, 201